ABOUT
FACE

ABOUT FACE

"A Wake-Up Call for the Church"

Pastor Joseph R. Trapani

XULON PRESS

Xulon Press
2301 Lucien Way #415
Maitland, FL 32751
407.339.4217
www.xulonpress.com

© 2022 by Pastor Joseph R. Trapani

Contribution by: Barbara Afanador and Rev James Houchens

Unless otherwise indicated, Scripture quotations taken from the King James
Version (KJV)–*public domain*

Personal images were donated by US Army Veterans, Joseph Trapani,
Gabriel Afanador, and Barbara Afanador. All other chapter images were
purchased through Canva.

Paperback ISBN-13: 978-1-66284-732-5
Ebook ISBN-13: 978-1-66284-733-2

THIS BOOK IS DEDICATED TO...

God in Christ Jesus who spared my life in more ways than one. He saved my life taking all the penalty for my sin on Himself giving me eternal life because death had no dominion over Him. There was no sin IN HIM, but your sin and my sin came ON HIM, if you believe. Even though a believer is dressed in civilian clothes he must not forget he is a soldier of light in a world of darkness. We were put here to make disciples of the Lord Jesus Christ. All Christian believers have been given a high calling by the LORD God Almighty. We are commanded to fight spiritual battles for the eternal souls of men. Your Captain is none other than the Lord Jesus Christ. He has equipped you with weapons which give life and not take life.

WORD OF WARNING:

THIS BOOK CONTAINS A GREAT DEAL OF SCRIPTURE AND SCRIPTURE WILL CHANGE YOUR LIFE AND THE WAY YOU LIVE.

TABLE OF CONTENTS

TIME TO RETURN TO THE WORD OF GOD

INTRODUCTION

For more than forty years I have been saddened when **I see former Christian Soldiers** and other veterans of prior wars struggling with life. They were once courageous and disciplined soldiers. Now many of these soldiers have surrendered their discipline, their courage, their valor, their integrity, their dignity and the honor they once possessed. They have allowed the enemy of their souls to gain ground and defeat them. They have succumbed and stepped "Outside the Perimeter" into enemy territory and he has captured them and placed them in dungeons of despair, hopelessness and complacency. They have become POW's (Prisoners of War). The dignity they once had which enabled them to hold their chest out and heads high has now been turned to shame. Today their heads hang in defeat. They live life in total sorrow; they are frustrated, disappointed, discontented, and unsatisfied. They are now marching to a different captain. Satan has taken them away through candy-coated booby traps of drugs, alcohol, lust, sex, etc. The devil has marched them far away from the true Captain Jesus Christ. He has tempted them and has drawn them away by Lust leading to Sin bringing them to the pinnacle of Death, the L.S.D. of their souls. They are now on a merciless bad trip. *(See James 1:14-15).*

This book is written to let the Christian soldiers know that **they can use both carnal and spiritual military tactics and insights** to make an "About Face" in their lives and once again return to God. If they would step back "Inside the Perimeter" of God's Word to be protected by Him, as they once again effectively use their shield of faith and their sword of the Spirit. Inside the perimeter of God, they will be able to reclaim their courage then fasten their bootstraps, salvage their integrity and "Forward March" with self-respect and in obedience to their Commanding Officer and Captain Jesus Christ. They must hear the Words of their Captain once again. As He cries "I Want You!" "About Face Soldier." Then they can re-enlist no matter what their age, no matter what they have done in their lives or with their lives. They can put on their uniform being fully equipped, and then stand at attention humbly yet proudly with their chest out and head held high. You can be Soldiers of Light in the Army of the Living God! *"For everything that is born of God overcomes the world, and this is the victory that overcomes the world, OUR FAITH." 1 John 5:4.* **Therefore, soldier it's About Face Time – Wake Up… "At-ten-hut Soldier…ABOUT FACE."**

Therefore, this book is an invitation to all believers to return from being Absent With Out Leave {A.W.O.L.} in God's Army. The Lord is calling.

Joshua 5:14-15 KJV And He said, "Nay; but as Captain of the host of the LORD am I now come. And Joshua fell on his face to the earth, and did worship, and said unto Him, What saith my Lord unto his servant? {15} And the Captain of the LORD'S host said unto Joshua, Loose thy shoe from off thy foot; for the place whereon thou standest is holy. And Joshua did so."

This book then is written in obedience to the Lord Jesus Christ who prompted me over the years to write what a Christian soldier may experience and has learned from both carnal and spiritual warfare that takes place in a person's lifetime. Many Christians have forgotten that they are soldiers in God's earthly army. THIS IS A WAKE-UP CALL FOR THOSE WHO HAVE FORGOTTEN. Being a Born-Again Christian pastor, I have taught several classes and preached sermons to try to call to attention the soldiers of Christ who are sleeping in the light of the "Glorious Gospel" of Jesus Christ. *"Thou therefore endure hardness, as a good soldier of Jesus Christ. {4} No man that warreth entangleth himself with the affairs of this life; that he may please him who hath chosen him to be a soldier. 2 Timothy 2:3-4 KJV*

Again, I must tell you most believers have forgotten that **"We Are Soldiers"** in Christ's army. We fight not with physical weapons but spiritual weapons that bring about eternal life, and not physical death. My children used to sing in church hymns like this one, "Onward Christian Soldier" by Sabine Baring-Gould. There are other songs, similar to this one reminding us we are soldiers of Christ as does the Scriptures themselves.

As illustrated on the cover of this book even though a Christian is dressed in civilian clothes, we must never forget we are soldiers for Christ, fighting the conflicts left over from Our Lord Jesus Christ's victory here on earth. **What then has happened? In this book "About Face,"** you are about to find out and **awaken once again and fall head over heels back into the Savior's arms or hopefully meet Him for the first time.**

"ABOUT FACE"
"Becoming A Victorious Christian Soldier"

Chapter 1

REPENTANCE

Christian, do you realize you are a soldier of Christ and that your captain Jesus Christ is the most exceedingly decorated and greatly honored Captain of all times? When his fellow soldiers deserted Him, He continued to fight. It was the "War of All Ages." In this battle He took a hill called Calvary, in the mountains of Moriah, by Himself! There He clashed with the enemy of all mankind and within hours He crushed the enemy's head, shattered his teeth and ripped out his claws. He fought to the end with only His Words, which will stand forever. With his very last breath on that hill the "War of All Ages" was won. To Him, all men owe a debt that we could never repay. Our spiritual freedom and eternal life were accomplished there, for those who chose to believe in Him. Our victory lies there at Calvary's hill. It is in Jesus Christ that you can be a victorious Christian soldier mirroring our Captain. Someone once said, **"We WERE Soldiers"**? No, the correct answer is, **"We ARE Soldiers."** Our Captain is none other than Jesus Christ the Messiah who fought not with weapons of this world but heavenly spiritual weapons. Thus, shall the Christian soldier fight with heavenly spiritual weapons not of this world.

The following chapters are written to let the Christian soldiers know that they can use military tactics and insights from the Word of God to generate an "About Face" in their lives and once again return to God by stepping back "Inside the Perimeter" of God's Word and be protected by Him with effective use of their faith in Him. Inside the perimeter of God they will be able to reclaim their courage then fasten their bootstraps, salvage their integrity and "Forward March" with self-respect and in obedience to their Commanding Officer Jesus Christ. They must hear the Words of their Captain once again. He screams "I Want You!" 'About Face Soldier.' They can then re-enlist no matter what their age, no matter what they have done in their lives or with their lives. They can put on the uniform of their Captain Jesus and His righteousness then once again be fully equipped standing proudly at attention with their chest out and head held high. You can be Soldiers of Light in the Army of the Living God whose blazing light shines in the darkness and the darkness will never be able to put it out. *"For whatsoever is born of God overcometh the world: and this is the victory that overcometh the world, even our faith." (1 John 5:4 KJV)* Therefore…"At-ten-hut Soldier…ABOUT FACE."

The church today must once again realize that every Christian is a spiritual soldier and must awake out of our slumber. Vacation time is over, there is much work to be done. Rest and Relaxation (R & R) will take place when Christ's kingdom comes to the earth. The average Christian has forgotten we are involved in a cosmic war, a war between God and Satan, a war between good and evil. This war has been going on for thousands of years. It's not a seven-day war not even a seven-year war it's the "War of All Ages." You were "born again" into this "War of All Ages" being selected, as soldiers of Christ but you must now be trained in spiritual warfare.

These chapters are designed to do just that! Notice that Paul addresses Timothy as a soldier, "*Thou therefore endure hardness, as a good soldier of Jesus Christ.*" 2 Timothy 2:3 KJV. Often, we forget that Jesus himself was and is a soldier with the rank of Captain. Proof lies in the Word of God, "*And it came to pass, when Joshua was by Jericho, that he lifted up his eyes and looked, and behold, there stood a man over against him with his sword drawn in his hand: and Joshua went unto him, and said unto him, Art thou for us, or for our adversaries? And he said, Nay; but as captain of the host of the LORD am I now come. And Joshua fell on his face to the earth, and did worship, and said unto him, What saith my Lord unto his servant? And the Captain of the LORD'S host said unto Joshua, Loose thy shoe from off thy foot; for the place whereon thou standest is holy. And Joshua did so.*" Joshua 5:13-15 KJV. This passage is known as a Christophany, a pre-incarnate appearance of Jesus Christ where He explicitly tells us He is the Captain of the armies of heaven.

These eight chapters are intended to allow you to envision yourself as a spiritual soldier. Not a soldier carrying destructive earthly weapons but a razor-sharp two-edged sword which is the Word of God. This sword brings eternal life to everyone it pierces. There are more than 31,000 verses (swords) within the framework of the Word of God. Every soldier must become highly skilled at using this sword. Learning to handle this blade accurately will empower you to become a victorious Christian soldier. "*For the word of God is quick, and powerful, and sharper than any two-edged sword, piercing even to the dividing asunder of soul and spirit, and of the joints and marrow, and is a discerner of the thoughts and intents of the heart." (Hebrews 4:12 KJV)*

These former soldiers including some believing Christian soldiers who hang their heads in anguish and despair can once again be brave, valiant, fearless men and women. They have lost their discipline, self-control, their zeal, their bravery, and their fight. They need to assemble around their Captain once again.

He has not abandoned them in their trials and tribulations. The United States Marines, like Jesus promises never to leave anyone behind or forsake them. See {Deuteronomy 31:6} *"Jesus Christ the same yesterday, and today, and foreever." (Hebrews 13:8 KJV)* It was Peter who deserted Jesus not Jesus who deserted Peter. The soldier of Christ must remember; you are not alone in this battle. Captain Jesus is always with you.

Have you ever noticed that a captain is typically the highest-ranking field officer? Therefore, a captain is highly respected and esteemed by his men; for this reason, He fights right alongside his men. This is a picture being painted of the Lord always being with you.

The first step once a soldier falls is to get on your knees. A soldier is never taller than when on his knees. Many examples of this are found throughout Scripture. One such example is found in… *2 Kings 6:8-23* where there was a plot by the king of Aram to capture Elisha. It was well known that the LORD told Elisha the military strategies of the king of Aram before they attacked Israel. Therefore, the king of Aram wanted Elisha eliminated. It was told to the king that Elisha was in the city of Dothan. As a result, this king sent horses and chariots and a great army to the city by night then surrounded it. In the morning, a great army surrounded the city and Elisha's servant was very fearful, but Elisha had prayed and said… *"do not be afraid there are more with us than with them."* Then the eyes of Elisha's servant were opened and he saw the mountains all around them were full of chariots and horses of fire. Take note of this; in battle it may look like you are losing but you must remember your Captain Jesus is with you in the battle. You may even appear to be losing but you are not. The Lord may be leading the enemy into a trap. His presence is always in the battle with you, reason being; if He does not go with you, how will anyone ever know you are not like other soldiers on the earth? *See Exodus 33:14-16.*

Unknowingly Daniel was also faced with a battle, and he prayed for 21 days yet no answer. He thought that God was not hearing him until an angel came and gave him insight and understanding. Little did Daniel know that the "War of all Ages" was raging in the heavenlies. Clearly the forces of darkness were putting up an effective fight against the Armies of the Light. However, it was Daniel's prayers to the LORD that were unleashing reinforcement angelic troops led by Michael the chief warring archangel. These angelic forces then took down the prince of Persia at that time, which was the dark principality over the Persian Empire. Evil was forced to stand down after many days. Some battles take days, some weeks and some even take years before the victory emerges, but remember the answer is in process. There is no doubt, Captain Jesus hears your prayers and initiates His battle strategy before the prayer comes out of your heart.

Isaiah records the Assyrian King Sennacherib's advancement upon Jerusalem during the reign of King Hezekiah of Judah. Sennacherib had just destroyed the ten Northern tribes of Israel (722 BC) and took them captive to Assyria. The righteous King Hezekiah put first things first; he took Sennacherib's letter before the LORD and prayed. God then put a hook in Sennacherib's nose and a bridle on his arrogant lips and sent him back by the way he came but not before…"*Then the angel of the LORD went forth, and smote in the camp of the Assyrians a hundred and fourscore and five thousand {185,000}: and when they arose early in the morning, behold, they were all dead corpses. So Sennacherib king of Assyria departed, and went and returned, and dwelt at Nineveh.*" *Isaiah 37:36-37 KJV.* King Sennacherib went back to Assyria with his tail between his legs only to be slain by his two sons Adrammelech and Sharezer as he worshipped his false god Nisroch. King Hezekiah called upon the name of the LORD his God and Captain Jesus directed the decisive blow that defeated the Assyrian troops.

THERE IS NO ROOM FOR COMPLACENCY in the armies of God, yet the Christian church is sitting in contentment and satisfaction. They are too comfortable and slack, and they have forgotten a cosmic war is raging round about them. They have misplaced their weapons for lack of use. Many soldiers in the church have taken off the breastplate of Christ's righteousness and abused God's grace. Their belt of truth has loosened and they are about to expose themselves. They have underestimated their enemy and like Goliath who had most likely taken off his helmet, so has the Christian soldier taken off the helmet of salvation guarding the influx of immoral material, and their shield of faith lies hopelessly beside their bed of complacency. Their sword of the Spirit, the Word of God, is dull from lack of use and sometimes just left at home. They swing the sword wildly instead of accurately with the skill of a musketeer. The church is in want of a repentant world, but the world is looking at the church waiting for us to repent. The same things take place within the church's walls. We look virtually like the world; the soldier of Light is surrounded by darkness due to the absence of personal righteousness, because many Christian soldiers have laid aside God's armour. *"For you were called to freedom, brethren; only do not use your freedom as an opportunity for the flesh, but through love be servants of one another." (Galatians 5:13 RSV).* The result is weakness because they have no offensive or defensive weapons available with which they can fight the forces of darkness. Let me illustrate. I know a soldier who was sent outside the camp during the Vietnam War, this soldier did not wear his helmet, left his M-16 and bayonet behind and no longer took a fellow soldier with him to ride shotgun, he traveled these roads through these villages dozens of times never having a problem. He had forgotten that he was in a war and complacency had set in. He never had any problems until one day when he was unprepared, then came the clacking of an AK-47 automatic. As the AK-47 rounds whistled all around him all he could do was put the pedal to the metal and hightail out of there. This soldier became complacent, and it almost cost him his life. Complacency can destroy a soldier and a soldier's effectiveness. You guessed it right, it was me who was that complacent, foolish young soldier. This is one of the reasons why I have been called to author this book.

ABSOLUTE SURRENDER. The soldier of Christ must be unquestionably surrendered to Captain Jesus. He must dispose of his double mindedness. Answer this question; is the Lord with you or not? Scripture is clear; He is always with you. In some areas of our lives, we walk in victory yet in other areas we walk in defeat. If you accept defeat, then that is what you will get since you put no effort into the battle. Your mindset must be secure in knowing that Captain Jesus already won the war. The Christian soldier cannot be double minded *(James 1:8)* otherwise he will be insecure in all his ways. The Greek word here for double-minded is "Dipsuchos –dip'-soo-khos," this actually means divided in interest and can even go as far as double souled. If your soul is divided, you must admit, you have a problem! Even the great King David understood this and asked the LORD to *"...give me an undivided heart, that I may fear your name" Psalm 86:11 NIV.*

I am praying that through God in Christ, we soldiers can once again pull up our bootstraps and be ready to stand tall, attentive to God with our head up, chest out and totally surrendered to God as brave, courageous, and fearless soldiers of Christ.

Joshua was told by Captain Jesus twice at the beginning of his offensive to take the Promised Land to *"be strong and of good courage". {Joshua 1:6-7 KJV}.* Joshua also gave this command to Israel just before his death for Israel to... *"... choose you this day whom ye will serve; whether the gods which your fathers served that were on the other side of the flood, or the gods of the Amorites, in whose land ye dwell: but as for me and my house, we will serve the LORD." Joshua 24:15 KJV.* There was absolutely no compromising in Joshua's life, nor should there be in ours.

YOUR RESPONSIBILITY IS TO PUT ON THE UNIFORM OF YOUR CAPTAIN. If you have at one time enlisted to be a soldier of Christ but have ventured outside of the perimeter of God, then you must admit your failure and re-enlist . *"Repent ye therefore, and be converted, that your sins may be blotted out, when the times of refreshing shall come from the presence of the Lord,"* (*Acts 3:19 KJV*) On the other hand, if you have never enlisted and turned your life over to Captain Jesus then you must sign-up. GOD WANTS YOU; therefore Chapter 1 "About Face" is for both of you. Give your life to Captain Jesus and you will never go wrong.

All soldiers of God must wear the uniform God has designed for them. You must put on Christ. *(See Romans 13:14)* Let me illustrate: A shepherd has two mother sheep, and both have given birth, one mother's little ewe lamb died at birth and the other mother sheep died in the process of birth. The shepherd now has a problem; he has a ewe lamb without a mother and a mother without a ewe lamb. The shepherd then takes the live ewe lamb and presents it to the mother sheep that has lost her little lamb. The mother sheep sniffs the baby and does not recognize the smell then she just walks away and will not nourish the baby lamb. The little lamb will die if it is not nourished. At this point the shepherd does something amazing: He takes the little ewe lamb which has died then skins it, next he ties the hide around the little lamb that has lost its mother and again the shepherd presents the baby lamb with the hide attached before the mother sheep. This time the mother sheep sniffs the baby lamb, and she recognizes the hide and the aroma and immediately she begins to nourish the little ewe lamb. Here is the parallel: The shepherd put the uniform of the dead ewe lamb over the live ewe lamb. Now the little lamb has the fragrance of the mother's dead baby lamb. *Ephesians 5:2* tells us that we are the *"aroma of Christ"* therefore we must put on Christ righteousness the armor of light. *(See Romans 13:14)* When we do this, God recognizes us as His own, wearing His uniform of righteousness and the fragrance of Christ is around about us. *"For we are unto God a sweet savour of Christ, in them that are saved, and in them that perish: 2 Corinthians 2:15 KJV.* You need the breastplate (uniform) of Christ's righteousness. Put on Christ and "ABOUT

FACE" (turn around) to head in the LORD'S direction. In other words, we are clothed in the righteousness of Christ having put on the robe of His righteousness. Let me back this up with another Scripture for confirmation; *"...my soul shall be joyful in my God; for he hath clothed me with the garments of salvation, he hath covered me with the robe of righteousness," ...Isaiah 61:10 KJV.*

Actually, there are hundreds "About Faces" in the Scriptures, let me name a few ...

1. In *Genesis 35:1-4* we see that Jacob ordered his entire household to wash and change their clothes and put away their false gods, their idols and he buried them under the oak at Shechem. Jacob was serious about his commitment to follow the one and only God.

2. After the LORD parted the Red Sea and the Hebrews crossed on the dry land, the people Moses led began to sing unto the Lord a new song. *Exodus 15:1-2 KJV "Then sang Moses and the children of Israel this song unto the LORD, and spake, saying, I will sing unto the LORD, for he hath triumphed gloriously: the horse and his rider hath he thrown into the sea. The LORD is my strength and song, and he is become my salvation: he is my God, and I will prepare him an habitation; my father's God, and I will exalt him."* The Hebrew nation did an "About Face" when they saw the LORD part the Red Sea. They were trapped between two mountain ranges one on their left and one on their right and the Red Sea preventing them from moving forward as the Egyptian army closed in from the rear. Pharaoh thought he would finally have his great slaughter but instead the LORD had His way that day when the Red Sea closed in on the Egyptians. Both Egyptians and Israelites began to fear the LORD knowing that Israel's God is God.

3. Samuel was told by the LORD to tell the people to put away their false gods and to prepare their hearts to serve the true God. Israel needed to make an "About Face." *See 1 Samuel 7:3-6*

4. On several occasions when David was king, Israel "About Faced" as the Ark of the Covenant was brought into the City of Jerusalem. *See 1 Chronicles 15:16.* Another time was when King David dedicated the materials for the construction of the Temple. Not to mention; David himself needed to repent and return to the LORD several times during his life.

5. Still another "About Face" took place in Israel at the dedication of the Temple that King Solomon had built. *"Now when Solomon had made an end of praying, the fire came down from heaven, and consumed the burnt offering and the sacrifices; and the glory of the LORD filled the house. And the priests could not enter into the house of the LORD, because the glory of the LORD had filled the LORD'S house. And when all the children of Israel saw how the fire came down, and the glory of the LORD upon the house, they bowed themselves with their faces to the ground upon the pavement, and worshipped, and praised the LORD, saying, For he is good; for his mercy endureth forever." 2 Chronicles 7: 1-3 KJV*

6. Israel again accomplished an "About Face" when Asa was king. King Asa of Judah was victorious over the mighty Ethiopian army, but God spoke to King Asa through the prophet Azariah on how important it was for Judah to abide in Him and not forsake the LORD. He then removed the detestable idols from all the land of Judah and from the cities of Benjamin. He also removed his own mother from queen and destroyed her idols at the Kidron Brook. *2 Chronicles 15: 1-4.*

7. Revival took place when King Jehoshaphat cleansed the temple and ordered the sanctification of all the Levitical priests. *2 Chronicles 19-20*

8. In the 7ᵗʰ year of Jehoiada the priest, King Jehoash (Joash) was presented to the people after Queen Athaliah had killed all the royal heirs and proclaimed herself queen. *"And Jehoiada made a covenant between the LORD and the king and the people, that they should be the LORD'S people; between the king also and the people." (2 Kings 11:17 KJV).* They repented and returned to the LORD as long as Jehoiada remained priest under King Jehoash. This is another "About Face" of the people of God.

9. The heathen city of Nineveh accomplished an "About Face" when Jonah preached after having a revival in his own heart as he spent three days in the belly of a great fish. *(Jonah 3)* Listen up church: revivals start in your heart first before it spreads to your neighbor when they see you make an "About Face." John Knox the great revival preacher of Scotland said to the LORD: "Give me Scotland or I die." Nobody ever tells us that God did answer that prayer with these words: "First die (to yourself) then I will give you Scotland." *And he said to them all, If any man will come after me, let him deny himself, and take up his cross daily, and follow me. Luke 9:23 KJV.*

10. Then revival again when King Hezekiah ascended to the throne and once more the temple was cleansed along with the people. *2 Chronicles 29-30*

11. Manasseh the wicked king of Judah who reigned for 55 years made an "About Face" in the last years of his life then tried to undo all the evil he did. *"And he took away the strange gods, and the idol out of the house of the LORD, and all the altars that he had*

built in the mount of the house of the LORD, and in Jerusalem, and cast them out of the city. And he repaired the altar of the LORD, and sacrificed thereon peace offerings and thank offerings, and commanded Judah to serve the LORD God of Israel. ." 2 Chronicles 33:15-16 KJV. Manasseh was the son of the righteous king Hezekiah. This is a testimony to the promised truth written in the Word of God. *"Train up a child in the way he should go, and when he is old he will not depart from it." Proverbs 22:6 KJV.* Parents don't ever fret; if you instructed your children in the way of the LORD then someday, they will return to the LORD. Pray that it be sooner rather than later.

12. When Ezra preached at the gates of the newly built walls in Jerusalem following Judah's return to Jerusalem after their 70 year deportation into Babylon (586 BC), there was another revival. *Ezra 9-10; Nehemiah 13*

13. Revival was once again beginning when the last Old Testament prophet John the Baptist arrived after 400 years of silence from the LORD. The people's repentant hearts led to the remission of their sins. *John Chapters 1*

14. People repented when Peter preached at Pentecost and 3,000 men turned from their sin and were saved. *Acts 2*

15. A couple more "About Faces" took place with the Samaritan women at the well in *John 4* and one in *Acts 8* when Phillip preached to the Ethiopian eunuch.

16. Many people in the city of Ephesus repented and turned to the Lord Jesus as Paul preached. *Acts 19* These people who practiced magic repented; confessing their practices and brought their books of magic together and burned them in the sight of

everyone. The burned books earthly value was of no importance anymore even though they had in today's market value a total of about 7.5 million dollars (based on daily wage of one hundred and fifty dollars per day). These Ephesian believers were sincere in their commitment to the Living God and it became a confession before the entire heathen city of Ephesus that they believed that Jesus Christ was the Messiah who paid the penalty for their sins and rose from the dead. They were headed in the wrong direction; however, they were given the order to "About Face" and they began service to the Lord Jesus Christ instead of serving devils that lay behind their occult practices. *Acts 19:11-21*

There are more "About Faces" in the Old and New Testament Scriptures. My prayer is that in these days there will be many more repentant hearts. More than just an "About Face" of unconverted people but also a change of direction for the believer who needs to repent in certain areas of his life and then make an "About Face." *"Now I rejoice, **not that ye were made sorry, but that ye sorrowed to repentance:** 2 Corinthians 7:9 KJV*

ABSOLUTE COMMITMENT is a necessity for the victorious Christian soldier. Josiah was a king who had absolute commitment to the LORD. When the book of law of Moses was found in the temple of the LORD, he did what was right in the sight of the LORD. According to *2 Chronicles 34*, King Josiah walked in his father David's footsteps seeing as he did not turn to the left or to the right. No doublemindedness here. He kept his focus on the LORD God of Israel. Josiah modeled what Jesus said was the greatest and foremost commandment; *"you shall love the LORD your God with all your heart, with all your soul, and with all your mind."* The Scripture tells us this of King Josiah… *"And like unto him was there no king before him, that turned to the LORD with all his heart, and with all his soul, and with all his might, according to all the law of Moses; neither after him arose there any like him." 2 Kings 23:25 KJV*

Having an absolute undivided commitment to the LORD requires focus on the LORD. If you are unwavering in your commitment, the things of this world will surprisingly become dim. Due to King Josiah's total commitment to the LORD, Israel completed another "About Face" as he led the nation. As the leader goes, so goes the nation, as the pastor goes, so goes the church, as the dad goes, so goes the family. *"Examine yourselves, whether ye be in the faith; prove your own selves. Know ye not your own selves, how that Jesus Christ is in you, except ye be reprobates?"* 2 *Corinthians 13:5 KJV*

Make a self-assessment and ask yourself in which direction you are leading those around you?

ABSOLUTE CLEANSING is a necessity for the triumphant soldier of Christ. Josiah was only eight years old when he became king and when he was sixteen and still a young man, he began to seek the LORD. He ordered all idols to be taken out of the temple. When the book of Mosaic Law was found in the temple after the 77 years of the unrighteous reigns of the kings Manasseh and Amon, King Josiah began to institute what had been lost and forgotten in Israel. *"And the king stood by a pillar, and made a covenant before the LORD, to walk after the LORD, and to keep his commandments and his testimonies and his statutes with all their heart and all their soul, to perform the words of this covenant that were written in this book. And all the people stood to the covenant."* 2 *Kings 23:3 KJV.* At age twenty he began to remove the high places from all Judah. He smashed the carved wooden images and the molded images into powder and scattered it on the graves of those who had sacrificed to idols. King Josiah meant business. He was so zealous for the LORD; he made a covenant and then reinstituted the Passover once again. In Biblical times covenants were made with the blood of a sacrificed unblemished animal. Captain Jesus, the Lamb of God instituted the New Covenant with His unblemished blood. Covenants are not contracts; covenants require blood, our Captain Jesus went all the way. Accordingly, all soldiers of Christ must stand firm for and in the Covenant, Christ paid for with his blood.

"And he put down the idolatrous priests, whom the kings of Judah had ordained to burn incense in the high places in the cities of Judah, and in the places round about Jerusalem; them also that burned incense unto Baal, to the sun, and to the moon, and to the planets, and to all the host of heaven.

And he brought out the grove from the house of the LORD, without Jerusalem, unto the brook Kidron, and burned it at the brook Kidron, and stamped it small to powder, and cast the powder thereof upon the graves of the children of the people. ." 2 Kings 23:5-6 KJV

Do you believe this? There were idols and idolatrous priests performing sacrifices to these idols inside the temple of God. Disgusting don't you think? King Josiah was so appalled that he did according to the law of Moses, *"And he slew all the priests of the high places that were there upon the altars, and burned men's bones upon them, and returned to Jerusalem." 2 Kings 23:20 KJV*

These priests have gone so far as child sacrifices as seen in verse 10…*" that no man might make his son or his daughter to pass through the fire to Molech."* The image was the body of a man and a bull's head with outstretched arms, it was made of metal then was heated to red-hot and the children were placed on the idol's arms. Gross, repulsive, and extremely nauseating and then we wonder why God told Joshua to wipe out all these people groups. The answer lies here; because the LORD knew they would lead His people astray to do horrific abominations. The LORD was protecting the nation of Israel, His children just as you would protect your children. Messiah would come through this people group someday. This is why God wanted these people wiped out.

<u>ABSOLUTELY NO COMPROMISE</u> is also necessary for the conquering Christian soldier. Josiah would have none of this and he meant business to clean up the temple, himself and the people of God. There was no compromising to serving anyone but the LORD. To be sure of this *2 Kings 23:20* tells us he went with his men to supervise the destruction of Baal and Asherah worship. Think of this; the king of

Judah got off his throne and did it himself; he wanted to make sure it was done. The bigger picture here is that the Old Testament Temple is a shadow of the New Testament truth that each of us is now the temple of the Holy Spirit. He dwells in us now. Like Josiah, the Christian soldier of Christ must be willing to clean-out his temple allowing no enemy to ensnare us or have a stronghold over us holding us captive to do his will instead of the LORD'S will. That's right; you are the temple of the Holy Spirit!!! *See 1 Corinthians 3:16; 1 Corinthians 6:19.* Cleaning out the temple may be painful but bearable and necessary.

This not only went on in King Josiah's day, but it still goes on today. Really you say! I saw this firsthand in Guatemala. There is a large so-called Christian church in a particular city that I visited twice on two separate trips. As I walked up the steps there were many fires burning. I asked the missionary, what is this? To my surprise he said they were witches who would offer prayers if you paid them. I was in deep disbelief, appalled and sick to my stomach. It only got worse from there, as our team entered the vestibule inside the church. There we found another fire with a male witch offering prayers for money. We were horror-struck at this point. How could the priests allow this to happen? I can relate to King Josiah, we wanted to extinguish their fire and throw them out the door and down the steps on their ears but instead we marched around the interior of the church seven times binding and rebuking evil spirits in the name of our Lord Jesus Christ, asking that this place be filled with the Presence of the Holy Spirit. How could this happen, I thought to myself, this a so-called Christian Church? It happened with the Temple in Jerusalem. It is what happens today in both the sanctuary building and the temple of the Holy Spirit, our body. If the soldiers of Christ do not give their temple completely to the LORD, then don't be surprised if the enemy gets a stronghold in the outer and inner courts of the temple in which you live.

If you have stepped outside the perimeter of the boundaries of God, you therefore need to turn around and head back into God's direction. Outside the perimeter the enemy has set up booby traps in strategic places to rob you of God's blessings. There is NO other way out of the enemy's POW camp (Prisoners Of War). There is only one way out. Captain Jesus calls out to you, "ABOUT FACE" and REPENT SOLDIER. Gather up your courage, son and "Forward March." Pick up your shield of faith in Christ and the sword of the Spirit and fight your way back to the "Stronghold of God." YOU CAN DO IT! You are strong and very courageous. You must go as David did against Goliath. He received the victory not because he fought well but because he BELIEVED WELL in God his Savior. You must conquer your Goliath. Your fellow soldiers are awaiting you in the church where you will be encouraged, refreshed, and on fire for the LORD once again.

You cannot have true faith in Christ without repentance. Therefore, heed your Captain and carry out His orders – "REPENT make an ABOUT FACE and RE-UP at once and RETURN to the LORD'S Camp.

Make it official and <u>SIGN</u> below with <u>ALL YOUR HEART</u>. Keep for your records because this is an important day.

Signature _____ Date _____.

"BASIC TRAINING"
"Becoming a Disciplined Christian Soldier"

TRAIN LIKE A SOLDIER OF CHRIST

Chapter 2

DISCIPLESHIP

On June 6, 1943, General Dwight Eisenhower spearheaded an assault against Adolf Hitler. One hundred sixty thousand British, Canadian, French and American troops; 800 aircraft, 5,000 ships, 13,000 paratroopers invaded five beachfronts on the north shores of Normandy, France. When they had reached the five beachfronts the German army was waiting for them. What if, as soon as the boats had reached the shore, the front door came down and out came a group of unarmed militia dressed in their olive drab boxer shorts wiping the fatigue from their eyes? If that were what really happened; the German soldiers would have laughed their socks off and they would have had target practice all day long. Fortunately, these soldiers that were storming the beachfronts were well trained and very brave; they had studied their enemy. They had trained extensively and pushed themselves to their maximum limit, becoming sufficiently qualified and highly prepared troops. Due to their training these soldiers were dressed in their battle gear and well outfitted with everything necessary to put up a good fight against the enemy. They were wide-awake and ready for battle. Their helmets were on their heads; their weapons were in their hands and their bayonet at their side prepared for whatever came next. They had the supplies and ammunition necessary to accomplish their assignment. Nevertheless, there were 10,000 casualties but there could have been 160,000 fatalities. This was the beginning of the end for Adolf Hitler and his German forces.

Sometimes I wonder if the Christian soldier is dressed for battle. The church as a whole needs a wake-up call to realize we are at war. May I ask you a question? Are most of the Christian soldiers you know really dressed in the armor of the living God? God's armor is a one-size fits-all battle gear. His armor is not like the armor King Saul was offering David to use while fighting the nine feet six-inch-tall Philistine giant Goliath. God's armor is not encumbering, it is especially adapted to each and everyone's size. When the Christian soldier marches out into the world, this is what we are to wear: God's armor! I challenge you to find me a Scripture telling us to take off the armor of God. Did you know God himself dresses in battle armor? *"For he {God} put on righteousness as a breastplate, and an helmet of salvation upon his head; and he put on the garments of vengeance for clothing, and was clad with zeal as a cloke." Isaiah 59:17 KJV.* Did you also know that Jesus had twelve disciples with Him and one of them was a betrayer?

Think about it? The enemy is in our camp. The world would call them a double agent or spy. Jesus addressed them as tares among the wheat.

The only way you can recognize them is by their fruit. Therefore, it is just good strategy, coupled with Godly wisdom, to wear your battle gear at all times. I know a soldier who was ordered to go outside the perimeter of the base camp in Sha Rang Valley, Vietnam to DaNang during the Vietnam conflict. However, he did not think to take his M-16. He thought, no big deal; I'm flying from one air base to another. Little did he know he had to get to another base camp once he arrived at the landing strip in DaNang. Because of this he had to venture alone through enemy territory with no weapon. Sounds foolish yet many Christian soldiers do this countless times. Like this soldier, we forget we are involved in the "War of all Ages" and that this war rages 24 hours a day, 365 days per year. God's protection was shown to this soldier when he arrived at the DaNang outpost. God had placed at the gate an MP which he knew. This MP made sure he supplied him with an M-16. You may be new at this type of warfare, but the enemy has been at war against God and his people for thousands of years. Therefore, the enemy has a decisive advantage over you unless we heed the orders of our Captain Jesus Christ, saying "Aye-Aye Captain" as we keep the armor of God on always as we proceed into the battle front.

"Put on the whole armour of God, that ye may be able to stand against the wiles of the devil. For we wrestle not against flesh and blood, but against principalities, against powers, against the rulers of the darkness of this world, against spiritual wickedness in high places. Wherefore take unto you the whole armour of God, that ye may be able to withstand in the evil day, and having done all, to stand." Stand therefore..." Ephesians 6:11-14 KJV

The spiritual soldier must know and understand how he is dressed in the spiritual realm. You must put on your spiritual eyes seeing the way in which God has dressed us. *Ephesians 6:11* God says; *"Put on the **whole armor** of God,"* Not just the pieces that you prefer but the **"whole"** armor of God.

2 Samuel 11:1-5 tells us King David stayed back at base camp in a time when the kings went off to war. Therein lays the trouble: David left the battle and took off his breastplate of righteousness laying it aside. Obviously, his helmet was off his head also, allowing the lust of the eyes, the lust of the flesh and pride to enter in as he gazed upon a beautiful woman taking a bath on the roof of a nearby building. "After all he thought, am I not the King of Israel?" The Christian soldiers, life is not a playground; it is a battleground for the souls of men.

When Paul wrote this passage in *Ephesians 6:11-17*, I believe he was thinking about the attire of the Roman soldiers with whom he had spent many years being chained beside.

(v.12) "For we wrestle not against flesh and blood, but against principalities, against powers, against the rulers of the darkness of this world, against spiritual wickedness in high places." (Ephesians 6:12 KJV.) Principalities are demonic forces over regions and territories. Daniel Chapter 10 tells us of a prince over the kingdom of Persia. Little did Daniel know there was war raging in the heavenlies until an angel stood before him and told him of this war in the heavens. *"But the prince of the kingdom of Persia withstood me one and twenty days: but, lo, Michael, one of the chief princes, came to help me; and I remained there with the kings of Persia." Daniel 10:13 KJV.* Looking deeper into this passage you see that this angel told Daniel that Michael, one of Captain Jesus' warring archangels came with troop reinforcements.

Our lesson here is to radio the Captain for Him to send reinforcements. How do we do this, through prayer. The problem was not that God did not hear the prayers of Daniel; it was the effective fighting strategy of the principality over the area that delayed the answer. There are principalities and powers over cities, states, and countries and even churches; therefore, pray fervently soldier of Christ, radio your Captain to send reinforcements.

Another reason you need the armor in place is because this war takes place even *"in the heavenly places." (Ephesians 6:12)* I personally have seen three senior pastors fall to the enemy's strategies. The enemy always wants the officers first. I know from experience that in carnal warfare; officers are not saluted in a war zone. Why, you ask? Snipers are always looking for the leaders to eliminate them knowing that will stifle the unit. The lesson here is you must protect your pastors and leaders by covering them in prayer. You must be *"praying always with all prayer and supplication in the spirit,"* prayer is your radio communication with your Captain, and be specific. Pray to the Lord to send reinforcements.

You have the authority to cancel enemy assignments over you. *"No weapon that is formed against thee shall prosper; and every tongue that shall rise against thee in judgment thou shalt condemn. This is the heritage of the servants of the LORD, and their righteousness is of me, saith the LORD."* *Isaiah 54:17 KJV*

Any tongue that rises up against you to accuse you as you serve the Captain, is of the devil and this verse tells us we have the authority to condemn him, he has no authority to condemn us. *"There is therefore now no condemnation to them which are in Christ Jesus, who walk not after the flesh, but after the Spirit." Romans 8:1.* Peter tells us in *(1 Peter 5:8 NASB)* that the enemy prowls around **'like'** a roaring lion. **He did not say he was a roaring lion.** If they rise up against you, this verse tells you that you are able to condemn them because our inheritance is in the LORD Himself and we are justified by the LORD. You must remember this…You are God's children. If the enemy isn't moving out of your way then our Captain Jesus has another purpose. He may be allowing it to build our faith and our character. Job's faith was challenged by his young friend Eliphaz in *Job 4:3-7 KJV.* *"Behold, thou hast instructed many, and thou hast strengthened the weak hands. Thy words have upholden him that was falling, and thou hast strengthened the feeble knees. But now it {trouble} is come upon thee, and thou faintest; it toucheth thee, and thou art troubled. Is not this thy fear, thy confidence, thy hope, and the uprightness of thy ways? Remember, I pray thee, whoever perished, being innocent? or where were the righteous cut off?"* It was now Job's time to exercise his faith and do what he had told others to do. Faith and character were being built here. The Lord may also be leading the enemy into an ambush for all you know! God had a purpose in allowing Joshua to be defeated at Ai. One was his lack of radio communication (prayer) to ask his Captain should he go. Pride showed its ugly face as Joshua had a great victory over his first campaign at Jericho.

Not to mention the sin of Achan *(Joshua 7)*. Another reason was to teach Joshua good battle strategy through a defeat. Joshua learned quickly; then on his second attack at Ai Joshua knew exactly how to draw the enemy warriors out of the city. There he flanked them on two sides and sent a third unit in from the rear and wiped out the city as God had ordered. Joshua studied his enemy's line of attack. The soldier of Christ must do the same.

(v.13b) "...having done all, to stand (14) Stand therefore, having girded your waist with truth, having put on the breastplate of righteousness, (15) and having shod your feet with the preparation of the gospel of peace; (16) above all, taking the shield of faith with which, you will be able to and quench all the fiery darts of the wicked one. (17) And take the helmet of salvation, and the sword of the Spirit, which is the word of God; (18) praying always with all prayer and supplication in the Spirit, being watchful to this end with all perseverance and supplication for all the saints—Ephesians 6:14-18 KJV

(v.13b-14a)"...having done all, to stand. (14) Stand therefore." Look at the forcefulness of these verses. They are emphatic, "to stand / stand therefore" God is driving this home. In other words, this is important. Do not be moved soldier of Christ. *"Every word of God is pure: he is a shield unto them that put their trust in him." (Proverbs 30: 5 KJV)* The Christian soldier must be unwavering, fixed and steady because God has spoken. It will come to pass, and you will be able to withstand in the evil day. Learn what you must learn soldier, and forward march double time.

(v.14b) having girded your waist with truth, this is the (belt of truth and it has several purposes. One purpose is moving forward very quickly by pulling the skirt up and tucking it into the belt for being able to charge when necessary. The Christian soldier must also pull up

his bootstraps and lay aside anything that encumbers us for battle. (See Hebrews 12:1). Peter tells us to gird up our loins revealing another purpose of the belt. The soldier's weapons such as the sword and dagger for the front-line foot soldier was attached to this belt. Also, for the archer the belt held the arrow quiver in place as they marched upon an enemy troop. In the modern army the bayonet and the handgun are attached to the belt. Most importantly Paul is telling us that God's word is the truth. If you do not gird your waist with truth, then do not be alarmed when your unrighteousness is indecently exposed. A further benefit is…if your waist is girded with God's truth then the enemy will be clearly identified.

(v.14c) having put on the breastplate of righteousness, this is the righteousness of Christ being put on which is talked about here. We have no righteousness before God apart from the blood of Christ. This breastplate protects our vital organs, especially the heart. It is written: *"Above all else, guard your heart, for it is the wellspring of life." Proverbs 4:23 NIV.* Apart from this we are commanded to be holy for He is Holy. We are not to continue in sin and abuse God's grace.

You must be wearing the wedding clothes of your Captain. *"Then saith he to his servants, The wedding is ready, but they which were bidden were not worthy. Go ye therefore into the highways, and as many as ye shall find, bid to the marriage. So those servants went out into the highways, and gathered together all as many as they found, both bad and good: and the wedding was furnished with guests. And when the king came in to see the guests, he saw there a man which had not on a wedding garment: And he saith unto him, Friend, how camest thou in hither not having a wedding garment? And he was speechless. Then said the king to the servants, Bind him hand and foot, and take him away, and cast him into outer darkness; there shall be weeping and gnashing of teeth. For many are called, but few are chosen." Matthew 22:8-14 KJV.* This is a parable of telling how you must enter heaven. You must be born again. See *John 3:3-7.* If you are born again, you are the righteousness of Christ. A backslidden Christian is out of fellowship, but still a child of God. Repentance returns him to righteousness. The righteousness of Christ is our wedding garments. We will not make it on our righteousness. We need Captain Jesus' breastplate of righteousness. *"I will greatly rejoice in the LORD, my soul shall be joyful in my God; for he hath clothed me with the garments of salvation, he hath covered me with the robe of righteousness, as a bridegroom decketh himself with ornaments, and as a bride adorneth herself with her jewels." Isaiah 61:10 KJV.* Good works will be the biproduct of wearing the breastplate. You will not be saved and enter heaven by good works. To think otherwise is to insult Jesus Himself by saying His work on the cross was not enough. We do good works because we love Him since He willingly laid down His life to save us. *See Titus 3:5-6 / Ephesians 2:8-9 KJV. "Jesus answered and said unto them, **This is the work of God, that ye believe on him whom he hath sent." John 6:29 KJV.** And this is the will of him that sent me, that everyone which seeth the Son, and believeth on him, may have everlasting life: and I will raise him up at the last day. John 6:40 KJV*

*{v.15} **having shod your feet with the preparation of the gospel of peace.",** 2 Kings 7:3-14* tells of four lepers who had good news but were hesitant to tell it…. but we will speak more of this in Chapter 8. The feet are especially important to the Christian soldier. A soldier cannot fight if his feet are not cared for properly. In the days of the Roman soldiers the enemy would plant pieces of glass and metal in the battlefield the night before, if the soldiers' feet are not protected by his sandals, he would be rendered useless for battle. Your feet must be sturdy when attacking in battle and a firm foundation is always necessary to the warrior. The Vietnam soldiers were taken out and rendered ineffective when they did not care for their feet due to the monsoons that soaked the land for months. Soldiers must always protect their feet and God has given you shoes to protect your feet as you share the good news of the gospel that God has commissioned us to carry.

*{v.16} **above all, taking the shield of faith with which, you will be able to quench all the fiery darts of the wicked one.*** The Romans soldiers had a shield like this, it was approximately 4 feet by 2 feet. You

undoubtedly have seen in Roman or Greek war movies as in the movie 300, when the Greeks went to battle against king Nebuchadnezzar, the enemy would shoot the arrows in the air and soldiers being attacked would work in unity with one another. The front lines would put their shields side to side, tight, and the soldiers in the middle would hold their shields up in the air so when the arrows came down, they would hit the shields giving them an umbrella protection from the enemy's arrows. The devil does the same thing; he likes to throw arrows of fire. The Romans would also water saturate the leather cover over their shield, and they would wet it before they went to battle, and it would stop the fiery darts and extinguish them. Hence, the unity of an army working together will be protecting one another and saving lives. The enemy of man's soul threw a few at Eve in the garden, and she did not hold up her shield of faith in God's Word. Satan defeated her there with the fiery dart of **"DOUBT"**... *"did God really say?"* The second fiery dart was **"DENIAL"**...*"surely you won't die."* And the third fiery dart was **"DECEPTION"**...*"God knows that if you eat of that fruit, you will become like Him."* The enemy loves to throw fiery darts and these three are the greatest, doubt, denial and deception. So don't be deceived, the shield provides shelter and of course we know that in Psalm 91 it says, *"he who dwells in the shelter of the Most High, will abide in the shadow of the Almighty."* In essence the shield protects you as you are hidden in God's shadow. Any soldier of Christ can claim this verse, "IF"you ABIDE and DWELL in the Most High.

{v.17a} *take the helmet of salvation for protecting your mind. Do not be transformed by this world but by the renewing of your mind.* The helmet of salvation protects our minds from the enemy lies. It protects our hearing also and our eyes. Goliath underestimated the enemy, probably removed his helmet and David slammed him between the eyes with a stone. The Bible says, the stone sank into his forehead, most likely the nose guard was absent allowing me to think that Goliath removed his helmet underestimating the LORD God of Israel and David. Therefore, you must study your enemy, and study how he works, not because you like him but because you want to effectively war against him. Hence, the helmet of salvation protects our heads, our minds, our ears, and our eyes.

{v.17b} take up the sword of the Spirit, which is the word of God. Now, the word, "WORD" in this passage in the Greek means (Rhema). *"In the beginning was the Word and the Word was with God and the Word was God." John 1:1 KJV.* The Word there is the Greek word 'logos', (the hand that created) but here we are talking, take up the Sword of the Spirit which is the word of God. Actually, the word Rhema means sayings of God. In the KJV Bible there are 31,102 verses of Scripture, you do not have to use the whole Bible against him, you can just take one verse out of the Bible in context and use it against the enemy. Therefore, you have 31,102 swords that you can use. When Jesus fought the enemy in the wilderness, he used the shield of faith and the sword of the Spirit. The enemy cannot stand the quoting of the Word of God. You must fight with the Sword of the Spirit. *2 Timothy 2:15 KJV, "Study to shew thyself approved unto God, a workman that needeth not to be ashamed, rightly dividing the word of truth."* We are talking about the Word of God here and the handling of it accurately. We are talking about not taking the sword and just swinging it wildly, if you whip your sword around, you are most likely going to hit something, but you are not going to be effective. You must take the sword of the Spirit, study it, and show yourself able and equipped to use the Word of God accurately. Jesus used the word of God accurately against the devil in the wilderness, and all the verses Jesus used, came out of the sixth and eight chapter of the book of Deuteronomy.

Very skilled is what we need to be when it comes to using the word of God, so how do we handle it accurately?

There are seven ways I can see: Deuteronomy said you have to #1) **read** the Word of God all the days of your life, #2) Joshua said you have to **meditate** on it, so that you are careful to do everything in it and make your way prosperous and have success, #3) Jeremiah said you have to **eat** his word and it will become the delight of your heart, not literally eating the Bible but to Spiritually ingest it. #4) Paul said to **hear** the word of God because faith comes by hearing, and hearing by the word of God, #5) Timothy was told by Paul to **study** {pay attention}, show yourself approved, and #6) Peter said to **grow** in grace and knowledge of Jesus Christ, and #7) Jesus himself said in Revelation 2, you have left your first love. **We must fall back in love with Jesus** and turn back to our first love. I mentioned earlier that God himself wears his armor when He goes to battle. *(Isaiah 59:17). "He put on righteousness like a breastplate, and a helmet of salvation on his head; and he put on garments of vengeance for clothing and wrapped Himself with zeal as a mantle."* This is a reference to God Almighty! God also puts on his armor; you must remember He is coming out of a righteous kingdom. He can take off His armor in the Kingdom, but if He goes to battle, He must have His armor on. The Christian soldier lives in a spiritual battle every day; therefore, we must always keep our armor on, never take it off. Nowhere in the Scriptures will you find a verse that tells you to take off the armor of God. We are in battle 24 / 7, 365.25 days per year. And why do you put this armor on? In order that you may stand against the wiles and deceptions of the enemy. You must remember that the devil has been around for generations and centuries, he knows how to make men fall.

{18a} **praying always with all prayer and supplication in the Spirit.** Our prayers are like a submarine shooting rockets up to heaven. We are now His ambassadors of the kingdom of heaven in a foreign country, doing God's work in a foreign land. How we communicate with Him is with prayer. The minute we take off our armor we become vulnerable to the enemy. We cannot leave a single item out. Take off your shoes and he will trip you up. Take off your breastplate of righteousness and your testimony is going to lose much spiritual weight. Take off your belt and you will be floating downstream with the rest of the fish. Let it be known; that "dead fish float downstream, live fish swim up." Many multitudes are floating downstream heading for the waterfall into the abyss. We were put here to stop them and to bring life to them using

29

the sword of the Word of God. We know that God has given to us all the weapons we need for victory." *2 Corinthians 10:3-5 NASB.* *"For though we walk in the flesh, we do not war according to the flesh, (4) for the weapons of our warfare are not of the flesh, but divinely powerful for the destruction of fortresses. (5) We are destroying speculations and every lofty thing raised up against the knowledge of God, and we are taking every thought captive to the obedience of Christ,"* NOTICE: God is on our side, the side of His Christian soldiers. When the Lord sent out the 70 disciples, they came back, *"...with joy, saying, Lord, even the devils are subject unto us through thy name. (18) And he said unto them, I beheld Satan as lightning fall from heaven. (19) Behold, I give unto you power to tread on serpents and scorpions, and over all the power of the enemy: and nothing shall by any means hurt you. (20) Notwithstanding in this rejoice not, that the spirits are subject unto you; but rather rejoice, because your names are written in heaven." Luke 10:17-20 KJV.* This is our agenda for rejoicing, your name is written in the Lamb's book of life."

The Life of the Christian Soldier must be...A Disciplined Life. When the soldier is in boot camp, he will learn discipline for every kind of battle he will face. Many believers have asked me what I think is the most valuable quality a Christian could possess? My answer is always...discipline. Discipline will carry with it consistency, self-control, character, and perseverance. At Boot Camp the soldier will be tested in every way imaginable developing restraint with boundaries. Many Christian soldiers immediately dislike their drill sergeants. The drill sergeants push these new recruits ridiculously hard, beyond their limits and with little or no encouragement. The recruits hated the discipline he was teaching them until they end up in the battlefield. Now they see why their drill sergeant pushed so hard. They were teaching them how to stay alive. They will not regret it later as he was teaching them survival in warfare. After the battle many soldiers finally appreciated their drill sergeants. We the soldiers of Christ long to kiss our Captain Jesus Christ for making it possible for us to make it through the trial of life. Most soldiers thought the drill sergeant was being malicious. Instead, he was teaching them skills to save their lives. He taught them strength of mind and body enabling them to survive the battle. They remembered his words that champions are made when they can go no further yet they push themselves to the extreme giving them the edge over their enemy. The Apostle Paul was one of the most disciplined soldiers of Christ in the Scriptures writing these words to those who are suffering. *"And not only so, but we glory in tribulations also: knowing that tribulation worketh patience; And patience, experience; and experience, hope: And hope maketh not ashamed; because the love of God is shed abroad in our hearts by the Holy Ghost which is given unto us." Romans 5:3-5 KJV.* During the Apostle Paul's first missionary journey he was dragged outside the city of Lystra and stoned supposedly being dead.

Did this stop him? No, he marched right back to Lystra. His trials did not make him weaker, they made him stronger. So is the way of the disciplined soldier, it will not kill you it will only make you stronger.

The Life of the Christian Soldier must be...A Yielded Life. A soldier in Basic Training is a soldier who has yielded his life to Captain Jesus. This phase is a time of learning to yield. He is a soldier willing to be separated from his loved ones, his home and his friends for a time. He has surrendered his life to being trained as a spiritual soldier in the army of the Living God. He has taken a new direction and has made the "About Face." He is willing to become a new creation. God is about to do a new thing in his life. This soldier is in the beginning phase of "buffing up" his spiritual muscles. In Basic Training he will learn to grow up to be a disciplined man, a soldier with a purpose. A soldier with determination to press on toward the high calling he has received from his Captain Jesus Christ. Even his diet is about to change; he will learn to feast on the Words of God and apply them to his life. *"Thy words were found, and I did eat them; and thy word was unto me the joy and rejoicing of mine heart: for I am called by thy name, O LORD God of hosts." Jeremiah 15:16 KJV*

12 TRAITS OF A SOLDIER'S YIELDED LIFE

{2 Timothy 2:1-4 NASB}, "You therefore, my son, be strong in the grace that is in Christ Jesus. (2) The things which you have heard from me in the presence of many witnesses, entrust these to faithful men who will be able to teach others also. (3) Suffer hardship with me, as a good soldier of Christ Jesus. (4) No soldier in active service entangles himself in the affairs of everyday life, so that he may please the one who enlisted him as a soldier."

1. A Soldier Must Be Strong *(2 Timothy 2:1 KJV), "You therefore, my son, be strong in the grace that is in Christ Jesus."* Boot Camp will filter out weak soldiers or it will develop them. The Captain of the Hosts of the Army of the Lord told Joshua to be strong and very courageous. Joshua 1:6,7 and 9. God gives grace and strength to accomplish what He has called you to do. Yet we have a responsibility to be strong and courageous. You must be confident that He who began this work in you will complete it. He called you and He will give you the faith, strength and courage to finish it. He will polish you. His words will bring you encouragement. When you feel weak you must remember this... *"I can do all things through Christ who strengthens me." (Philippians 4:13 KJV).* So, a soldier must be strong, that's why he goes through boot camp to get developed, strong and courageous.

2. A Soldier Must Be Faithful To His Call, *"...entrust these to faithful men who will be able to teach others also." 2 Timothy 2:2.* Paul is telling Timothy to train other men. The work must go on. Each generation must train the next generation to be faithful men and soldiers of Christ. In order to train another in faithfulness you must be faithful. You are a living message to the next generation; those under your leadership, family, friends, and fellow soldiers are watching to see if you do what you say. Are you faithful to your Commanding Officer?

This is where I will mention Ittai the Gittite, I love his commitment to King David. I do not know if he was a believer in the LORD God of Israel, but I do know he was devoted to his king. Here is what happened, Ittai came to David and joined his army the day before Absalom, (David's son) drove him out of Jerusalem. Ittai had 600 men with him when Ittai joined David's army. The next day David and his loyal people are leaving the city and went down crossing the Kidron valley. There David stopped as he watched the people pass. Then here comes Ittai with his 600 men. David had many Philistine friends and Ittai and his 600 men were included amongst them. These were the oppressed and the poor who made up David's following, they were a rag tag team of soldiers. David saw Ittai coming and went up to him: *"Then said the king to Ittai the Gittite,"* Wherefore goest thou also with us? return to thy place, and abide with the king: for thou art a stranger, and also an exile. Whereas thou camest but yesterday, should I this day make thee go up and down with us? seeing I go whither I may, return thou, and take back thy brethren: mercy and truth be with thee."* I love Ittai's response, here is what he said *"And Ittai answered the king, and said, As the LORD liveth, and as my lord the king liveth, surely in what place my lord the king shall be, whether in death or life, even there also will thy servant be." 2 Samuel 15:20-21 KJV.*

Can we say that? Are you going to be that faithful to your commanding officer even if you joined yesterday?

3. A Soldier Must Be Able To Teach Others *2 Timothy 2:2 & 24 and 25 NASB.*

Vs 2…*" The things which you have heard from me in the presence of many witnesses, entrust these to faithful men who will be able to teach others also."*

Vs 24-25…*"And the servant of the Lord must not strive; but be gentle unto all men,* **apt to teach,** *patient, (25) "The Lord's bond-servant must not be quarrelsome, but be kind to all, able to teach, patient when wronged, (25)* *with gentleness correcting those who are in opposition, if perhaps God may grant them repentance leading to the knowledge of the truth,"*

Therefore, a soldier must be able to teach and be teachable. Moses spent 40 years in the desert learning humility, he was being taught by God. A soldier must be meek and humble. What does meek and humble have to do with being able to teach? The soldier who is able to be taught is one who can receive from another wise God-fearing man. Moses was meek {Numbers 12:3} and able to be taught even though he led Israel out of Egypt. God spent forty years training him in the land of Midian. I do not perceive him as a wimp because he was meek but a man of faith able to be taught and able to teach others. Joshua was humble, he was Moses' servant. *See Joshua 1:1.* He served Moses and was taught by him to serve the Lord for at least 40 years in the desert. He was a military leader, and he certainly was not a wimp. These men were teachable. These men did not place themselves above their brothers. They were approachable because they were teachable. Their fellow man could reach out to them regardless of their position. They had soft pliable hearts and because their hearts were soft they were teachable by God and men. God could use them because they were able to be molded by God, pliable in God's hands. A soldier must be teachable! A teacher is a learner, and a learner will inevitably become a teacher. Moses, Joshua, and many others in the Bible were meek not weak. Meekness and humility are strength under control.

4. A Soldier Must Endure Hardship. *(2 Timothy 2:3 NASB), "Suffer hardship with me, as a good soldier of Christ Jesus."* A soldier must endure hardship. Being a soldier is not a cakewalk, it is tough, you must to train extensively, you are going to be in places like Paul, he was shipwrecked, whipped, scourged, he was weary, he suffered pain, he was in the cold, in the heat, he was in hunger, he was in danger of vipers, but enduring hardship is part of a soldier's life. It also builds character and patience. Paul tells us in Romans those tribulations produce patience and patience experience and experience hope and hope does not disappoint.

I hope you did not think for one moment that being a soldier was easy. Soldiers endure difficulty. They are disciplined to obey, and this discipline will save their lives. They train extensively, every muscle they have is driven to its extreme. They at many times suffer pain, weariness, fatigue and exhaustion. On top of this they are in danger almost regularly. After Boot Camp many soldiers end up with orders for a hostile warzone and there he will learn to sleep with his weapons at all times. It could be humidly hot, it may rain for what seems to be months, and there may be vipers ready to ambush you. In Southeast Asia (Vietnam) there were vipers called the step and a half, and the other, the three step. Yep, you guessed it, with the one you were dead in a step and a half, and the other within three steps. Yes, there may be danger all around and snipers ready to pick you off at any time. You are trained to survive on the land or worse like eating C-rations for weeks at a time. I know soldiers who dropped massive amounts of weight and now they were in good physical strength. But a soldier is trained to be strong and disciplined to face this hardship. Most soldiers now, would love to thank their drill sergeants. Enduring hardship makes a soldier stronger, builds character and teaches patience. *"When He has tested me, I shall come forth as gold. Job 23:10 NASB*

5. A Soldier Must Avoid Entanglements With The World. *(2 Timothy 2:4 NASB), "No soldier in active service entangles himself in the affairs of everyday life, so that he may please the one who enlisted him."* When a soldier is in Boot Camp, he is forced into not being entangled with the world. He is in training and all distractions are removed. Soldiers are to be focused. They have one goal, the orders he has received from his Captain. Think of the British Royal Guard. You can stand in front of him, jump up and down, make funny faces yet he will not be distracted. Even with these distractions there is still no activity, yet his eyes are straight forward and motionless. He is highly trained and focused. Pick up a weapon to come against his guard and you will find yourself in great distress. He is not concerned with such action going on around him. He is only concerned with what would be detrimental to his assignment. Soldiers of Christ, do not be distracted by nonsense that interferes with your assignment to war against the enemy of our souls and to recruit fellow soldiers.

6). A Soldier Must Please His Commanding Officer *(2 Timothy 2:4 NASB) "so that he may please the one who enlisted him."*

If you, please your commander you will be rewarded. A free pass for the weekend or even the easiest job he can assign to you. No KP duty for you, your peeling potato days are over. You have pleased your Captain. I remember my tour of South Vietnam. It was December 1971. My unit was deactivated by President Nixon and many of us were going home. I was handed two sets of orders. One set told me to go down to Long Binh to be reassigned to a different unit in Vietnam. A few days later I received a second set of orders. This set of orders told me I was going home. I was greatly distraught! So I took both sets of orders to the first sergeant for the reason that my captain was wounded when his APC (Armored Personnel Carrier) hit a land mine months earlier. I was a radio operator and therefore I was always with the Captain, lieutenant and first sergeant. Because I had pleased my commanding officers and first sergeant, I was sent down to Headquarters in Long Binh with my first sergeant's signature on the set that would send me home. The orders to stay in South Vietnam were voided and the orders signed by my first sergeant were accepted sending me home. What a reward! Who knows where I would have ended up or if I even would have made it safely home? It is a good thing to please your commanding officer. Then someday we will hear Him say…" *Well done my good and faithful servant."*

7. A Soldier Must Be A Man of Integrity *(2 Timothy 2:5 KJV),* *"And if anyone competes in athletics, he is not crowned unless he competes according to the rules."* In the KJV, a soldier is identified as an athlete because who must be in top physical condition. The Basic Training, he must go through conditions him to endurance. An athlete must compete by the rules and so must a soldier. All six of the Roman centurions listed in the New Testament where men of integrity during the time of Christ. I'm sure all centurion soldiers are not honorable men, but a Christian soldier of Christ must be a man of good report.

The Roman centurions I would compare to a modern-day US Army Captain. He is a working-class officer just as Captain Jesus was and is today. He gives orders but he is also able to take orders from a higher-ranking officer and carries them out. In most cases the army captain is the highest-ranking field officer. He is right there with his men in the dirty work that must be accomplished to win the battle. His position was one of respect and admiration. They were the backbone of the Roman army. In the book of Joshua Chapter 5, we see a pre-incarnate appearance of Jesus Christ, this is known as a Christophany. Joshua fell and worshipped this Captain and took off his sandals because this ground was now Holy. We see that this is a Captain of a higher order army, the Captain of the Hosts of the Armies of the LORD. What is significant about this is that it shows that the Lord Jesus Christ is right with us in the heat of every battle we may face. The Captain never leaves us or forsakes us. Remember this when you are in battle against the world, the flesh and yes, even the devil, especially the devil. The Bible speaks favorably about these centurion soldiers, but we have no time to discuss them.

8. A Soldier Must Be A Student. *2 Timothy 2:15 KJV, "Study to shew thyself approved unto God, a workman that needeth not to be ashamed, rightly dividing the word of truth."*

In Boot Camp (Discipleship Training) you will be trained to use the issued spiritual weapons of warfare. A soldier of Christ is trained not for physical warfare but rather spiritual warfare. These weapons will be addressed as we move through this chapter.

"For the word of God is quick, and powerful, and sharper than any two-edged sword, piercing even to the dividing asunder of soul and spirit, and of the joints and marrow, and is a discerner of the thoughts and intents of the heart. Neither is there any creature that is not manifest in his sight: but all things are naked and opened unto the eyes of him with whom we have to do..." Hebrews 4:12-13 KJV. A soldier is educated to accurately use the

sword of the Spirit the Word of God. Again, I tell you a swordsman is not one who swings his sword wildly. He is one who handles his sword precisely and accurately. Have you ever watched one of the three musketeers handle a sword with extreme accuracy? They are so skilled with their sword that they can put one hand behind their back yet proficiently using their sword as an offensive and defensive weapon. They know precisely when to pierce the heart of their enemy. The soldier of God should be such a one. Not just waving the Word of God wildly but expertly and perfectly to let the Word of God judge the thoughts and intentions of the hearer's heart. As I mentioned earlier in Chapter 1 the *Word* in the phrase "sword of the Spirit which is the *Word* of God is the Greek word *"Rhema"* meaning the sayings of God. Again, let me remind you there are 31,102 verses in the Old and New Testaments of the KJV Bible. Each one is a saying of God. If you are student of God's Word, then it is at your discretion for you to skillfully use any one or any combination of God's swords to counteract the enemy's attacks.

9. A Soldier Must Be Steadfast *2 Tim. 2:19 NASB, "Nevertheless, the firm foundation of God stands, having this seal: "The Lord knows those who are His;" and, "Everyone who names the name of the Lord is to keep away from wickedness."*

God's Word is a solid foundation. The man of God must build his house upon a rock in this way the foundation is certain. The LORD is his rock and his fortress and his deliverer; his strength, in whom he trusts; The Lord is his shield and his stronghold. *"… my beloved brothers, be steadfast, immovable, always abounding in the work of the Lord, knowing that your labor is not without fruit in the Lord." 1 Corinthians 15:58 KJV*

10. A Soldier Must Be A Honorable Vessel God Can Use. *2 Timothy 2:20-21 KJV, "Now in a large house there are not only gold and silver implements, but also implements of wood and of earthenware, and some are for honor while others are for dishonor. (21) Therefore, if anyone cleanses himself from these things, he will be an implement for honor, sanctified, useful to the Master, prepared for every good work."*

You became an honorable vessel set apart and useful to the Captain when you received Jesus as Lord and Savior and changed directions turning away from your sins. It is important that you stay inside the perimeter by being compliant to your Captain until you are trained properly and assigned orders. We should not continue to sin and abuse the grace that was extended to us through faith. Scripture tells us.... *"For the flesh lusteth against the Spirit, and the Spirit against the flesh: and these are contrary the one to the other: so that ye cannot do the things that ye would". Galatians 5:17*

11. A Soldier Must Be In Good Spiritual Shape. *2 Timothy 2:22 NASB, "Now flee from youthful lusts and pursue righteousness, faith, love, and peace with those who call on the Lord from a pure heart."*

After King David was confronted about his youthful self-righteous lusts with Bathsheba by Nathan the prophet. He repented immediately and penned Psalm 51. He asked the LORD to *"Create in me a clean heart, O God, and renew a steadfast spirit within me.".* David knew he was in sin and his heart was impure. I looked at the Hebrew verb here for "create" to find out exactly what David was undergoing. The Hebrew verb used is "Bara" meaning 'create from nothing.' David's heart was unclean, and he preferred that his heart be re-created. Start over LORD because I have fallen from a great height due to my pride and lust. While you are at it LORD then... *"Restore in me a right spirit."* Application for the Christian soldier is to keep your heart pure and you will be in good spiritual shape. In other words, *"Watch over your heart with all diligence, for from it flows the springs of life." Proverbs 4:23 NASB*

12. A Soldier Must Be Patient. *2 Timothy 2:24-26 KJV, "The Lord's bond-servant must not be quarrelsome, but be kind to all, skillful in teaching, patient when wronged, (25) with gentleness correcting those who are in opposition, if perhaps God may grant them repentance leading to the knowledge of the truth, (26) and they may come to their senses and escape from the snare of the devil, having been held captive by him to do his will."*

Also *2 Timothy 2:6* talks about the farmer. We soldiers are to be like the farmer. A farmer is patient as he waits. First, he plows the ground, then he plants the seed. He waits on God to water it with rain and dew from heaven. Then he waits for the growth of the fruit from God's hands. We must have patience when we teach, we need not quarrel to pry people into the kingdom. We must wait as the farmer waits for the seed to take root and to grow and allow the seed to be watered until the Holy Spirit brings the revelatory knowledge of Christ to them. When they genuinely believe having the revelatory knowledge from God then they will be released from the trap in which the devil has them ensnared. At this point they will be soon delivered from the bars of sin that had imprisoned them. Patience is a weapon of God. If you wait long enough patience will force deception to reveal itself. Then you will be able to recognize and rebuke the devil and be released from the devil's snare.

Basic (Discipleship) Training is a Time of Learning *(Ephesians 6:11-18 NASB).* At the time of training the new soldier will be issued God's armor for his protection and spiritual warfare. He will be trained in using these weapons. Unlike David who was given King Saul's armor which did not fit but encumbered David in going to battle against Goliath. God has given us His armor and it is a "one size fits all" armor. It is especially adapted to each and every individual soldier.

"Put on the full armor of God, so that you will be able to stand firm against the schemes of the devil. (12) For our struggle is not against flesh and blood, but against the rulers, against the powers, against the world forces of this darkness, against the spiritual forces of wickedness in the heavenly places. (13) Therefore, take up the full armor of God, so that you will be able to resist on the evil day, and having done everything, to stand firm. (14) Stand firm therefore, having belted your waist with truth, and having put on the breastplate of righteousness, (15) and having strapped on your feet the preparation of the gospel of peace; (16) in addition to all, taking up the shield of faith with which you will be able to extinguish all the flaming arrows of the evil one. (17) And take the helmet of salvation and the sword of the Spirit, which is the word of God. (18) With every prayer and request, pray at all times in the Spirit, and with this in view, be alert with all per-severance and every request for all the saints," *Ephesians 6:11-18 KJV.*

Your Battle Equipment. A soldier is now living in a new environment. The former life you have known has been absolved. You live in a kingdom within a kingdom. God has given you equipment to live and move and have our being in this new world. God's equipment consists of several pieces that will make you an effective soldier.

First of all, remember this is God's armor and God's armor consists of...Belt of Truth, Breastplate of Righteousness, Sandals of the Gospel of Peace, Shield of Faith, Helmet of Salvation, Sword of the Spirit accompanied by Prayer and Supplication.

We are told to "put on" this equipment. *"Put on the full armor of God, so that you will be able to stand firm against the schemes of the devil." Ephesians 6:11 NASB.*

I know you want me to compare this to a Roman soldier, but you have heard that all before. Therefore, I will liken the soldier to a scuba diver who has been given the equipment to live in an atmosphere to which he does not belong. A scuba diver, how silly, this is a book about soldiers. Let me explain and then tell me if it is unreasonable. Think about this, a scuba diver finds himself in an environment where he does not belong, yet he swims and dives within and he can survive for a period of time. Likewise, when we were born again into God's realm we were born into a new environment. A kingdom in which we find ourselves unable to exist apart from our life source. We must have oxygen. The air we breathe enables us to survive in this foreign environment. The scuba diver has compressed air in his tanks and likewise the Holy Spirit enables us to breathe in this strange place. Yet we can dive into the deeper things of God and search for the beautiful pearls as we swim within.

God has given us goggles and now we can see clearly as He illuminates our surroundings and gives us understanding of why we are here in this new environment. We now have the understanding we are here to catch fish, dead fish, just floating around wherever the currents take them. We are called to wake them up before they wash over the falls into the abyss. We are called to catch them with our swords (the speargun) but this sword is the Word of God that does not take life

41

but rather it will give them eternal life. This sword enables us to save these dead fish, bringing them to eternal life in Christ Jesus before the sudden destruction that awaits them.

There is an enemy that hates what we are doing because he wants to feed on these dead fish. They are easier to devour this way. These predators also try to take us out. They love trying to chomp on our air lines to suffocate us from the Lord and His Word that feeds us air, food, and drink from above.

God has also issued us a wet suit (a shield and breastplate) if a predator tries to bite into it then his chomp has no effect. Our wet suit armor is too strong for him because every Word of God has been tested by the saints and God has become a shield for us. It is Christ's righteousness that keeps the enemy from tearing us apart.

We also have great mobility in this world as God has issued us flippers (shoes) and we can stay one step in front of these predators as we have been given speed in the wisdom from the Word to outwit them. These flippers enable us to take our message of the Good News to far reaching places. Some scuba soldiers swim in the shallows to catch top water fish. Other divers swim in mid-level waters to catch middle class fish. Some divers swim deep to catch intellectuals and explain to them the reasons God exists. God has His scuba divers in all levels of society. All we must do is adjust our weight belt that the believer may be found in any water level simply by adjusting the weights on his belt that he can bring the Word of Truth to the dead fish in any level.

All believers have a weight belt (belt of truth) that enables us to fish at any water level as we seek out dead fish in any stage of society to inject them with the truth of life. That Messiah has come into the world that He created to rescue men from sure and certain death by being swept over the falls into the place prepared for the devils and his angels of darkness.

Your head gear (helmet of salvation) will protect your mind from the enemy's lies. Your salvation will be secure in the assurance that you are God's and God is yours. He has equipped you to cast off the enemy's lies and hold fast to the truth. *"Isaiah 40:8 KJV "The grass withereth, the flower fadeth: but the word of our God shall stand forever."* His Word is a sure thing.

Do you still think I am out in left field? I think not. We have not moved; we are secure in Christ. The enemy is trying to move the playing field and men are following his deception. Scripture tells us not to move God's established boundaries. You must put on God's issued equipment or you will not survive in this alien place for very long. Leave off your battle gear and you will be as a wounded fish, easy prey for the predators of your soul, the devil and his evil associates of darkness.

Be wise, do not ever take your God given armor off (scuba gear). Remember my challenge in Chapter One. There is no verse of Scripture telling us to take off God's armor. Remember, Jesus had twelve disciples and we found out that one was influenced and led by the devil, obviously he was not wearing the armor God had provided for all believers, yet he fellowshipped as if he were a believer. Always leave your armor on, just in case because we never know.

Ephesians 6:18 KJV. "With all prayer and petition pray at all times in the Spirit, and with this in view, be on the alert with all perseverance and petition for all the saints."

Prayer and supplication are like radio transmissions to the Father. Many times, we do not have because we do not ask. We always need a helping hand, and the Lord is always there to help when we call. His power is at our beckoned call, even before it comes out of our mouths but as soon as it wells up in our hearts.

FOR YOUR INFORMATION

The Lord's cell # is… *Jeremiah 33:3 KJV "Call unto me, and I will answer thee, and shew thee great and mighty things, which thou knowest not."*

God in Christ is always there for you. CALL UPON HIM AT ANY TIME HE IS ALWAYS AVAILABLE.

"REVEILLE"
"Becoming an Obedient Christian Soldier"

HERE I AM LORD, SEND ME!

Chapter 3

CALL TO ATTENTION
TO WAKE UP

Do this, knowing the time, that it is already the hour for you to awaken from sleep; for now salvation is nearer to us than when we believed. (12) The night is almost gone, and the day is near. Therefore let us lay aside the deeds of darkness and put on the armor of light. (13) Let us behave properly as in the day, not in carousing and drunkenness, not in sexual promiscuity and sensuality, not in strife and jealousy. (14) But put on the Lord Jesus Christ and make no provision for the flesh in regard to its lusts. Romans 13:11-14 NASB

REVEILLE IS A WAKE-UP CALL TO REMEMBER, REPENT, RETURN TO YOUR FIRST LOVE AND DO YOUR FIRST WORKS

Every morning the soldier is awakened to the sound of the trumpet. This means you only have so much time to wake up, ready yourself and line up for headcount and formation. Here the soldier must stand at attention. Fully awake, his head held high, chest out, arms to the side and fully dressed and ready for the battle of the day. Night is over, it is now the call of awakening. Soldiers of Christ, one trumpet has already sounded. The angels herald it in the heavens as they said, *"for today in the city of David there has been born for you a Savior, who is Christ the Lord."*

The next trumpet is about to sound. The Light has come, and it is time to awake from sleep for the next trumpet will be this one written in Paul's letter to the Thessalonians. *"But I would not have you to be ignorant, brethren, concerning them which are asleep, that ye sorrow not, even as others which have no hope. (14) For if we believe that Jesus died and rose again, even so them also which sleep in Jesus will God bring with him. (15) For this we say unto you by the word of the Lord, that we which are alive and remain unto the coming of the Lord shall not prevent them which are asleep. (16) For the Lord himself shall descend from heaven with a shout, with the voice of the archangel, and with the trump of God: and the dead in Christ shall rise first: (17) Then we which are alive and remain shall be caught up together with them in the clouds, to meet the Lord in the air: and so shall we ever be with the Lord. (18) Wherefore comfort one another with these words." 1 Thessalonians 4:13-18 KJV*

You should already be dressed in the Armor of Light. If you are not in formation, you would be considered AWOL (Absent With Out Leave). The one who goes AWOL is classified as lazy or he is a deserter. While deserters lack courage the true soldier never quits. *God's soldiers are not of those who shrink back to destruction, but of those who have faith to the preserving of the soul. Hebrews 10:39 Paraphrased.* Many Christian soldiers are AWIL (Asleep With In the Light). This is not an option for a Christian soldier. When a soldier is sleeping; he cannot speak, he cannot hear, he cannot think, he cannot walk, he cannot fight, and he certainly is not able to obey his Captain. A soldier must always be ready. When the soldier is asleep, he is not prepared, and if you are not ready the enemy can defeat you easily and you will be caught off guard. The element of surprise is always the great advantage in battle.

Therefore, since morning has come, the Light of the world is here. Reveille has already taken place. You must take your place in formation and heed the commands of your Captain. Jesus had rallied His troops. It is the beginning of a new day, a new era. It is the beginning of the new covenant Jeremiah the prophet spoke of in Jeremiah 31:31. *"Behold, the days come, saith the LORD, that I will make a new covenant with the house of Israel, and with the house of Judah":* therefore, we are to be watchful, ready, and faithful to our Captains orders. Time is running out the next trumpet is about to sound, and man's salvation is nearer than when you first believed. *There is urgency about the time to awake out of sleep. The Apostle James tells us, "…behold, the Judge is standing right at the door. (James 5:9 NASB).* Paul also tells us, for the time is almost here. We cannot fall asleep, now is the day to speak of the salvation of our souls provided by Our Lord.

THE NEXT TRUMPET IS ABOUT TO SOUND

("For the Lord himself shall descend from heaven with a shout, with the voice of the archangel, and with the trump of God: (1 Thess. 4:16 KJV) See above.

This wake-up call needs to be preached in the church and us soldiers must be afraid no longer. Then and only then will the enemy's demonic foundations and evil strongholds be shattered. They will have no place to stand or grasp onto any longer and they will stumble to their destruction. The church will once again be triumphant. I think of those famous words of the Japanese Admiral Isoroku Yamamoto during World War II when he was congratulated on his victory at Pearl Harbor. He was quoted as saying…" I fear that we have awakened a sleeping giant." If the soldiers of Christ wake up from their slumber, it is the devil who will begin to fear because the church is that sleeping giant.

The trumpet of reveille has sounded on that holy night in Bethlehem. It is now the last hour and the next trumpet will soon sound. Soldiers of Christ you must get about our Captains business and wipe the drowsiness from your eyes. *"For this reason, the Word of God says, "Awake, sleeper, and arise from the dead, and Christ will shine on you." (Ephesians 5:14 NASB)* **"Atten-Hut soldiers!"** The night is over the Light has come.

ISRAEL'S CALL TO WAKE UP IS IDENTICAL TO THE CHURCH.

Isaiah 29:13-14 KJV "Wherefore the Lord said, Forasmuch as this people draw near me with their mouth, and with their lips do honour me, but have removed their heart far from me, and their fear toward me is taught by the precept of men: (14) Therefore, behold, I will proceed to do a marvellous work among this people, even a marvellous work and a wonder: for the wisdom of their wise men shall perish, and the understanding of their prudent men shall be hid."

The people of Israel had lost touch with their God; they only spoke unbelieving words of and to Him. They wanted only their traditions to be carried on. Their heart was far from Him. They had lost their first love. Since they had no heart, they were about to perish. The enemy was defeating them within their own ranks. He had infiltrated their service to God.

Likewise, the Christian soldiers must be careful and watch, the enemy is infiltrating the church. Many churches that began in the Spirit are now being perfected by the flesh. They have lost their first love. Now it is about tradition, religion and politics. Our Captain warned us of this. *"And he charged them, saying, take heed, beware of the leaven of the Pharisees (religion), and of the leaven of Herod (politics)." (Mark 8:15 KJV)* There it is in black and white on the pages of your Bible. Mark that in red in your Bible because Jesus specifically told us Himself. Churches have fallen and are falling by the swarms to enemy infiltration. Even the Lord had politics and religion infiltrate His twelve disciples, yet He did not allow it to get a foothold. This occurs when the word is not found in your heart since there is a loss of your first love for God the Father and your Captain Jesus Christ.

PILLOW PROPHETS PLAGUED ISRAEL

Even the prophets of Israel had lost touch with their God; they had fallen asleep. *"Wherefore thus saith the Lord GOD; Behold, I am against your pillows, wherewith ye there hunt the souls to make them fly, and I will tear them from your arms, and will let the souls go, even the souls that ye hunt to make them fly." (Ezekiel 13:20 KJV)*. In other words, I am against your traditions, legalism and religion.

The LORD was against these so-called shepherds who were destroying and scattering the sheep of God's pasture. Therefore, the LORD God of Israel said that since they have driven the people away from their God and have not attended to their spiritual needs that He would soon discipline them for their evil deeds. But the remnant the true believers that were left nonetheless still love Him. He will bring them back to the land He had given them. Then He would raise up a shepherd over them of whom they will not be terrified that would come from the righteous branch of David. It is He who will reign as their King. He will be called the LORD my righteousness.

TRUE PROPHETS JEREMIAH AND EZEKIEL OBEYING AND PROPHESYING THE WORD OF THE LORD:

Jeremiah 26:2-8 tells us, "Thus saith the LORD; Stand in the court of the LORD'S house, and speak unto all the cities of Judah, which come to worship in the LORD'S house, all the words that I command thee to speak unto them; diminish not a word: (3) If so be they will hearken, and turn every man from his evil way, that I may repent me of the evil, which I purpose to do unto them because of the evil of their doings. (4) And thou shalt say unto them, Thus saith the LORD; If ye will not hearken to me, to walk in my law, which I have set before you, (5) To hearken to the words of my servants the prophets, whom I sent unto you, both rising up early, and sending them, but ye have not hearkened;" {6} "Then will I make this house like Shiloh, and will make this city a curse to all the nations of the earth. (7) So the priests and the prophets and all the people heard Jeremiah speaking these words in the house of the LORD. (8) Now it came to pass, when Jeremiah had made an end of speaking all that the LORD had commanded him to speak unto all the people, that the priests and the prophets and all the people took him, saying, Thou shalt surely die." They wanted Jeremiah and Ezekiel dead. They were liars and murderers and did not know the LORD.

After the truth being told by Jeremiah, they plotted to murder him for his obedience to the LORD commands and planned on continuing in the tradition, legalism and politics.

AND FOR THEIR LACK OF
HEARING, GOD SAID:

Jeremiah.23:1-6 KJV "Woe be unto the pastors that destroy and scatter the sheep of my pasture! saith the LORD. (2) Therefore thus saith the LORD God of Israel against the pastors that feed my people; Ye have scattered my flock, and driven them away, and have not visited them: behold, I will visit upon you the evil of your doings, saith the LORD. (3) And I will gather the remnant of my flock out of all countries whither I have driven them, and will bring them again to their folds; and they shall be fruitful and increase. (4) And I will set up shepherds over them which shall feed them: and they shall fear no more, nor be dismayed, neither shall they be lacking, saith the LORD. (5) Behold, the days come, saith the LORD, that I will raise unto David a righteous Branch, and a King shall reign and prosper, and shall execute judgment and justice in the earth. (6) In his days Judah shall be saved, and Israel shall dwell safely: and this is his name whereby he shall be called, THE LORD OUR RIGHTEOUSNESS."

Jeremiah and Ezekiel were not asleep, they were wide awake to the LORD, and they spoke the words the LORD God told them to speak. Yet these pillow prophets continued a plot to murder them. God was appalled by this. The prophet Ezekiel was also horrified as the prophets prophesied from their own motivation and lied to the people who loved listening to their lies. Israel's prophets had developed an art of making God's people comfortable in their relationship to Him. They tickled Israel's ears with their lies and deception and half-truths. They left out justice, mercy and humility. Sound familiar? See *Ezekiel 13:17-19 NASB. "Now you, son of man, set your face against the daughters of your people who are prophesying from their own inspiration. Prophesy against them {18} and say, 'Thus says the Lord GOD, "Woe to the women who sew magic bands on all wrists and make veils for the heads of persons of every stature to hunt down lives! Will you hunt down the lives of My people, but preserve the lives of others for yourselves? {19} "For handfuls of barley and fragments of bread, you have profaned Me to My people to put to death some who should not die and to keep others alive who should not live, by your lying to My people who listen to lies."*

Isaiah was also sickened by the priests who led them astray and confused the direction of their paths. See *Isaiah 3:12.* The LORD God also cautions us today through the Apostle Paul to be watchful... *"Watch ye, stand in the faith; be men, be strong; 1 Corinthians16:13 YLT.* Since we interpret Scripture by Scripture here is more support. *"I charge you therefore before God and the Lord Jesus Christ, ... (verse 5) but you be watchful in all things, endure afflictions, do the work of an evangelist, fulfill your ministry." 2 Timothy 4:1 & 5 NKJV.*

If you are not watchful, guess what; you are not being wise, therefore watch, stand in faith, be men, be strong and stay alert. It can cost you severely if you are not. The soldier who falls asleep while on guard duty will find himself being court-martialed or cost the lives of many a soldier. I am sorry to say, many Christian soldiers are asleep for the most part. What damage we could do to enemy strongholds if we are awake in the battlefield bringing eternal life to them as we handle accurately the sword of the Spirit.

<u>GIVE ATTENTION UNTIL I RETURN...</u>

Till I come, give attendance to reading, to exhortation, to doctrine. (14) Neglect not the gift that is in thee, which was given thee by prophecy, with the laying on of the hands of the presbytery. (15) Meditate upon these things; give thyself wholly to them; that thy profiting may appear to all. (16) Take heed unto thyself, and unto the doctrine; continue in

them: for in doing this thou shalt both save thyself, and them
that hear thee. 1 Timothy 4:13-16 KJV

Daniel Webster defines complacency as contentment. I said earlier in this book that complacency kills. It sounds awfully harsh but it's true! Let me give you a good example from my life as a soldier in the US Army. I found myself in South Vietnam 1971. My unit was called the "Jungle Clearers." You perceived correctly we cleared the jungles in the Central Highlands from Viet Cong (VC), snipers and North Vietnamese soldiers (NVA). Let me remind you of what I brought up in Chapter 2, that I may drive the horrible consequences of complacency. I was young and foolish; I volunteered to make daily mail runs from our outpost to the air base about a forty-five-minute drive. I did this every day and sometimes twice per day. We the soldiers desperately needed to hear from home. When I first started this run every day, I would take my M-16, another man as my shotgun, plus a man in the back bed of the vehicle in case of attack. After doing this day after day, week after week and month after month never having a problem, I slowly began to go alone without a shotgun and man in the back. After many trips it ended up that I began to go alone, even forgetting my M-16, believing there would never be a problem. One day I as I was driving though a village outskirt, I began to hear the clack, clack, clack of an AK-47 and rounds whizzing over my head. Realizing I had left my M-16 behind I knew I was in deep trouble. I had only one option I put the pedal to the metal, or it was certain death or capture. I high tailed it as fast as I could to the Phu Cat Air Base. One hundred feet or so inside the airbase the engine froze solid. After being towed back to the field unit the motor pool sergeant was waiting to court martial me for not checking the oil in the truck before I left our base camp. But he soon found out that there was a hole in the oil pan draining out all the oil. I believe it was a ricocheting AK-47 round piercing the oil pan. It wasn't until seven years later, after coming to know Jesus Christ as my Captain that the Lord began to put this together. The LORD had protected me in my foolishness and has shown me how not to be complacent by using my military training in Christian warfare through applying the principles of God's Word to the spiritual battles against Satan and dark forces of evil. Being complacent is not wise for the soldier of Christ. The enemy is nearby to take you out and he most certainly will if you take off your battle armor and equipment. Again, I challenge you to find Scripture telling us to take off the armor of God, there are no Scriptures telling you to do so.

When you lay aside your spiritual weapons, the helmet of salvation, the breastplate of righteousness, the sword of the Spirit or any piece of God's issued armor. Then the enemy's flaming arrows will be able to catch you off guard and pierce you with many a pang. Our words are rendered inadequate to fight against the enemy of God, but God's Words extinguish enemy arrows that are shot strategically at us.

These pillow prophets are still with us today. They were in Jeremiah's day, they were in Jesus' day, and they are existent in today's day and age. Our Captain has given a charge for all pastors to preach sound doctrine.

"For the time will come when they will not endure sound doctrine; but after their own lusts shall they heap to themselves teachers, having itching ears; (4) And they shall turn away their ears from the truth, and shall be turned unto fables." 2 Timothy 4:3-4 KJV

The soldiers of Christ need to keep their focus on sound doctrine. The Captain gave us orders and we must not turn our ears from His command. Soldiers stay true to their Captain. Those who are side-tracked will not preach sound truth. They will say what they want to say and what men want to hear and do it for their own personal gain. They will tickle ears and strut around like roosters putting on a show. Where is the conviction of sin? Where is the confession of sin? Where is the repentance for sin? The Great revivals of the past were spearheaded by strong hell fire and brimstone teachings. Preachers like Jonathan Edwards and George Whitefield of the 1700's didn't mince their words and Biblical teachings. They stayed true to their Captain and half of the Boston area placed their faith in Captain Jesus. These men were not afraid to speak truth even if men did not want to hear the truth.

The church battalion in the ancient city of Ephesus lost sight. Jesus said to them… *"I know thy works, and thy labour, and thy patience, and how thou canst not bear them which are evil: and thou hast tried them which say they are apostles, and are not, and hast found them liars: (3) And hast borne, and hast patience, and for my name's sake hast laboured, and hast not fainted. (4) Nevertheless, I have somewhat against thee, because thou hast left thy first love. (5) Remember therefore from whence thou art fallen, and repent, and do the first works; or else I will come unto thee quickly, and will remove thy candlestick out of his place, except thou repent. Revelation 2:2-5 KJV*

THESE FOUR FACTORS WILL CAUSE YOU TO LOSE YOUR SHARP EDGE

1. Falling out of love with Jesus.

2. Forgetting how close you were with Christ in the beginning of your walk with Him.

3. You must Repent and Return to your Captain.

4. You must do the things you did at first, as crazy as it may have been. You really had faith then, didn't you? Ask yourself? Do you have more faith today than you did when you first believed in Christ?

The Ephesian Church had lost their first love and with that loss their razor-sharp cutting edge was gone. So, it is with many Christian soldiers today. They are no longer madly in love with their Captain Jesus Christ. They have ceased to use the sword of the Spirit and their edge had become dull. They had forgotten that the constant use of the sword of the Spirit will keep the sword sharpened.

Solomon tells us in *Ecclesiastics 10:10 GNB.* "If your ax is dull and you don't sharpen it, you have to work harder to use it. It is smarter to plan ahead and stay sharp." It is only wise to have a sharpened edge when cutting or else you will work much harder and still not accomplish the Captains objective. Remember *2 Kings Chapter 6?* The prophets had Elisha's permission to build more places for the sons of the prophets to stay. One of the prophets while cutting a tree lost a borrowed axe head which fell into the Jordan River. He had to stop cutting because the sharp edge was gone. He could have kept on hitting the tree trunk as hard as he could with the wooden handle and you would never hear the word, Timber!!! Elisha was told this then cut off a wooden stick and threw it into the water and the iron axe head floated to the surface. This is a picture of a Biblical truth. The wooden stick represents the cross of Captain Jesus, and He makes your work as easy as floating on eagles' wings. Staying true to the Scriptures is to stay sharp. With very little effort men, cities, nations, and continents will bow their knees to Captain Jesus. If you want your cutting edge back, you must apply the above four factors once again.

WAKE-UP & REMEMBER

You must remember or did you forget who Jesus is? Listen up soldier! *"He (Jesus) was in the world, and the world was made by him, and the world knew him not." (John 1:10 KJV).* The heavens are the work of His fingers. The stars are all numbered, and He calls them by their names, yet man cannot comprehend the quantity of them. The very earth on which we live is His footstool. Scientists tell us the earth spins on its 23.5-degree axis at 1,000 mph while it orbits the sun at a speed of 67,000 mph.

Mount Everest is 29,028 feet above sea level and the Mariana Trench in the South Pacific Ocean is 35,048 feet deep. If you went there, you would find He is there. Where then can you go from His presence? Believe it soldier, your Captain has everything under control.

Did the enemy divert your attention from this Biblical truth? That is who you are fighting against. *"Our struggle is not against flesh and blood..." (Ephesians 6:12 NASB)* The devil is always there and will try to divert your attention and distract you with things such as the lust of the flesh, the lust of the eyes and the boastful pride of life.

YOU MUST EXECUTE AN "ABOUT FACE"

About Face means to repent and forsake your sin, to turn around 180 degrees and march in the opposite direction. We are told there are at least 147 Bible verses concerning repentance which are found in KJV version of the Old and New Testament. *"And the times of this ignorance God winked at; but now commandeth all men everywhere to repent: (31) Because he hath appointed a day, in the which he will judge the world in righteousness by that man whom he hath ordained; whereof he hath given assurance unto all men, in that he hath raised him from the dead." Acts 13:30 & 31 KJV.* Jesus said it this way, *"I tell you, Nay: but, except ye repent, ye shall all likewise perish. (Luke 13:3 KJV)*

This is not sorrow or remorse but a forsaking of sin resulting in a sudden change in direction that has been initiated in your heart.

RETURN TO YOUR FIRST LOVE

The Christians here have not lost their love, they have simply drifted off from Him and have begun to love something else more. They have left Him; He did not leave them. You must recognize what caused your distraction, was it money, fame, prestige, success, alcohol, drugs, lusts, sex or was it one of many other sins that caused your downward slide? Realize you are in a battle. Your victory lies there as you fight the good fight of faith. Our God wants you to remember this... *"Do I have any pleasure in the death of the wicked,"* declares the Lord GOD, *"rather than that he should turn from his ways and live? (Ezekiel 18:23 NASB).* Then God reinforces this a few verses later in *Ezekiel 18:31 & 32.* *"Cast away from you all your transgressions which you have committed and make your-selves a new heart and a new spirit! For why will you die, O house of Israel? (32) "For I have no pleasure in the death of anyone who dies," declares the Lord GOD. "Therefore, repent and live."*

DID YOU FORGET WHAT JESUS DID FOR YOU?

The blood Jesus shed, His beard that was pulled out, the scourged flesh of His back and sides and we cannot forget that crown of thorns? Plus, His bruised face from being punched repeatedly while blind-folded. Oh my, and those nail pierced hands that did the work of the Father and the pierced feet that carried His Word.

Do you not recall the seven trials Jesus went through in one night? Three of them religious; one being Annas the Jewish high priest, the second Caiaphas, the Roman appointed high priest and then the trial before the Sanhedrin. He was found guilty at all three. You and I both know He was guiltless. Three more trials were civil trials, one before Pontius Pilate the Roman governor, the second civil trial before King Agrippa of the Jews and then back to Pontius Pilate again. The last trial was a spiritual trial before God the Father where He was found not guilty of sin and therefore sinless and spiritual death had no dominion over Him. Yes, it was the same day since it is today in the Kingdom of Heaven. We know this because of what Jesus said to the dying repen-tant criminal crucified beside Him.

Did you forget the earthquake, the thunder, and the lightning taking place as Jesus was dying on the cross? Remember the Roman Centurion who had seen hundreds of these crucifixions, witnessing these things cried out *"surely this was the Son of God."* Believe me he had never seen anything like this. *Colossians 1:16 KJV says, "For by him were all things created, that are in heaven, and that are in earth, visible and invisible, whether they be thrones, or dominions, or principalities, or powers:*

all things were created by him, and for him:" This centurion was seeing and perceiving that God's creation was mourning the physical death of this Man Jesus whose sign above Him read…"KING OF THE JEWS." John tells us in…*John 1:1–5 KJV "In the beginning was the Word, and the Word was with God, and the Word was God. (2) The same was in the beginning with God. (3) All were made by him; and without him was not anything made that was made. (4) In him was life; and the life was the light of men. (5) And the light shineth in darkness; and the darkness comprehended it not." (verse 14) And the Word was made flesh, and dwelt among us, (and we beheld his glory, the glory as of the only begotten of the Father full of grace and truth."*

Also bear in mind the layers of curtains in the temple being approximately 12 to 18 inch thick, being torn from top to bottom opening to ALL MEN the only access to Father God through Christ Jesus His Son.

Do not fail to remember His last words…

1. *"Father, forgive them for they know not what they do."*

2. *"Today, you will be with Me in paradise.*

3. *"Women, behold your son, son behold your mother."*

4. *"My God, My God, why have You forsaken Me?"*

5. *"I thirst."*

6. *"It is finished."*

7. *"Father into Your hands I commend My Spirit."*

I hope you did not forget the resurrection and His several appearances that were recorded? First to Mary in the Garden. Then to the women as they walked to report the empty tomb to the disciples. Then the two on the road to Emmaus, also His appearance in the upper room with Thomas being absent? Additionally, His appearance eight days later to the disciples with Thomas being present as Thomas declared Jesus was his Lord and God. (See John 20:28) Then Paul in 1 Corinthians 15:6 tells us of His appearing to over 500 at one time. Should I also mention He appeared to Peter and the disciples who witnessed His ascension in a cloud with the angels telling us He will come again in the same way?

Consider all but one Disciple died a Martyr's death. Would you die for a lie if it were not true? The disciples died a martyr's death because they knew the truth. The books from historical antiquity tell us of their courageous faith. James the brother of John was first to be martyred by a sword see Acts 12. Peter was crucified upside down. Thomas died by spear in India. Simon the zealot was sawed in half. Andrew passed being crucified on an X-shaped cross. Philip died also being crucified. Nathaniel (Bartholomew) departed this life flayed & then beheaded. Matthew was killed with halberd axe. James son of Alpheus was martyred being stoned & clubbed. Jude was clubbed then beheaded. Paul was beheaded in Rome by Caesar Nero. Stephen went to meet your maker as he saw Jesus standing at the right hand of the Father while being stoned, this being recorded in Acts Chapter 7. The Apostle John was boiled in oil but like the three Hebrew children that were not scorched by the fiery furnace, God spared John's life to bring us additional information recorded in the book of Revelation.

Are we missing something here? Why do we seem to have forgotten the reality of His existence? Where is our faith? Listen and put into practice your faith once again. *Hebrews 4:2 KJV... "For unto us was the gospel preached, as well as unto them: **but the word preached did not profit them, not being mixed with faith** in them that heard it."* In other words, our faith must be applied to God's Word for the believer to profit.

REMEMBER AND RETURN TO YOUR FIRST LOVE, YOUR LORD JESUS CHRIST.

Do you remember the day you received Him as Savior? Do you remember the burning in your heart, the forgiveness you received, the joy of your salvation, the brighter colors, and the beauty of God's creation and so much more? SOLDIER OF CHRIST, THINK BACK AND REMEMBER your prior victories through Christ in those days. He does the same today. *"Jesus Christ the same yesterday, and today, and forever." (Hebrews 13:8 KJV)*.

"A.I.T"
"Becoming A Skillful & Gifted Christian Soldier"

TRAIN IN THE WORD OF GOD

Chapter 4

A.I.T. "ADVANCED INSTRUCTIONAL TRAINING"

This chapter is Advanced Instructional Training (A.I.T). In the Armed forces you would go from Basic Training to your specialized Training.

In this chapter we will learn what gifts the Lord has given you. When you enter the Armed Forces, they test you to find out what you are gifted in. God has gifted you when you received Jesus Christ as your Lord and Savior, but you have other gifts that he has equipped you with. You need to find out what your gifts are and apply them to your Christian walk. Some of you are already moving in the gifts God has given you, some of you might need to step up or out into the gifts God has given.

We are going to investigate some of the spiritual gifts that God has equipped you with, this is your specialty God has given you as a warrior. In the U.S. Army it is called M.O.S. {Military Occupational Specialty}. These gifts have a purpose of bringing glory to the Lord and edify yourself and the church. Peter tells us in 2 Peter 3:18 KJV to grow in grace and knowledge of Our Lord Jesus Christ. This is what we are doing when we come to church and Bible studies, we are growing in the knowledge of our Lord Jesus Christ. We are commanded to grow, not I think you should. That is what A.I.T. achieves, when you are sent to Advanced Instructional Training (A.I.T.). Even the Apostle Paul tells Timothy along with us today that we must..." *Study to shew thyself approved unto God, a workman that needeth not to be ashamed, rightly dividing (handling accurately) the word of truth." (2 Timothy 2:15 KJV)*

You need to remember that we are in a war, and you are a soldier of Christ. We are not to be on R&R (Rest and Relaxation) all our allotted time here on earth. This is complacency, you have forgotten that the war between good and evil rages on. We are in a fire fight everyday with unseen forces of evil and you must be equipped for warfare. We fight this battle every day and it affects every person on the face of the earth. It is not warfare with people, this is cosmic warfare with forces of our enemy, the devil. There are two Kingdoms clashing being in conflict with one another. One Kingdom is under the command of our Captain Jesus Christ, the Prince of Peace (Psalm 103:19, Isaiah 9:6); the other kingdom is under the command of Satan, the prince of the Power of Darkness (Matthew 12:26; Colossians 1:13). You were born again into this battle. Our Lord Jesus Christ already won this war. We are just called to take back what was lost when mankind fell in the Garden of Eden. The New King James Version calls it the WILES of the enemy, meaning organized strategies. The devil has organized strategies against us, and he also has an organized battle plan. Satan and his forces have been around longer than mankind. If you have been around for more than 10,000 years like him, you would be a worldly scholar today. After 10,000 years of learning you would have a good handle on everything, but you have only been around a few years.

Satan has organized strategies against us and therein is the reason Jesus Christ sent His Holy Spirit. In this way we can fight against the enemy with God's wisdom.

The hierarchy of Satan's Kingdom is composed of "Principalities", they are Satan's head officers planning on how to defeat each of God's believing soldiers. The rulers mentioned are Satan's divisional commanders over cities, churches, homes, etc. The devil has organized strategies against us, and we must have the wisdom of God through the Holy Spirit to fight them. God has given us all gifts to help us win each battle we face.

Remember Chapter 1, when Jesus said, "I WANT YOU?" You answered and said yes, sign me up? You may or may not have known you were signing into a war that has been going on for ages. God gave you gifts when you were saved to help you in this battle.

Maybe you are in the infantry being a front-line soldier. Remember Uriah, Bathsheba's husband? He was placed in the front line by King David. David wanted him dead to claim Uriah's wife. In this way, he could hide his sin since she was pregnant with David's baby. Uriah was killed even though he was loyal to his king. Some of you are front-line soldiers and God will give you the gifts to accompany your battle assignment. This gift could be the discernment of spirits or discernment of evil or wrong teachings that come across churches.

Some of you may be an artillery soldier, you have the gifts of faith that can move mountains. God will move whatever it is in your way since there is no doubt in your heart. See *Mark 11:22-24 KJV. "And Jesus answering saith unto them, Have faith in God. {23} For verily I say unto you, that whosoever shall say unto this mountain, be thou removed, and be thou cast into the sea; and shall not doubt in his heart but shall believe that those things which he saith shall come to pass; he shall have whatsoever he saith. {24} Therefore I say unto you, what things soever ye desire, when ye pray, believe that ye receive them, and ye shall have them.*" **Notice this Scripture says…it is <u>you</u> being told to tell the mountain to move and not to ask God to move it. It is <u>your</u> faith that is at work here and the Lord promises to grant what you ask.**

Some of you may also have the gift of communication and be able to teach and preach in God's church.

The medics are the miracle workers, and God uses you to bring healing to the wounded Christian soldiers and get people back in the functioning spiritual position.

You may be a sniper and God uses you for a one on one evangelism. You may not be a Billy Graham, but every one of us is called to evangelize. Talking with them and enlisting others into God's army recruiting them. You may be doing that right now with your family and friends or even your neighbor.

A mechanic may be someone that restores people with the gifts of hospitality and encouragement. As Barnabas was to Saul when he knew Paul was truly saved and encouraged the apostles to accept him. Mechanics exhort others for they are a repairer of a broken vessel.

The office staff are more like administrative positions giving out orders, but they still are to participate in strategic warfare. Supply clerks are the ones who equip us, like your pastor or teachers. These are also equippers of the Word of God.

It is clear from Scripture that no position is any greater than the other. We all have one common purpose. 1.) to plant, 2.) to reap, and **these are one and the same and will be rewarded accordingly**. "*So then neither is he that planteth any thing, neither he that watereth; but God that giveth the increase. (8) Now he that planteth and he that watereth are one: and every man shall receive his own reward according to his own labour.*

"Now he that planteth and he that watereth are one: and every man shall receive his own reward according to his own labour." (1 Corinthians 3:7-8 KJV) No matter what position you hold in God's army, there should be no disunity. We will all be rewarded according to our investment.

Therefore, every part of the body of Christ should function in perfect order just like God's amazing design of the universe. The church must function in this way. The armies of God must operate in like manner. None of us believers have all the gifts to make up a functioning church by ourselves. We need one another and then the church will be victorious and prosper with additional recruits. One instrument out of tune in an orchestra can mess up the entire symphony. Every gift should be represented in each individual church, but that is not how it is in today's churches.

Therefore, we have one spiritual army with a variety of different gifts. There is to be no DISUNITY. Jesus told us a kingdom divided against itself cannot stand (See Mark 3:24) When I was in Vietnam, I was a radio operator. I was in communications with a combat engineer outfit, and we would go out and set up a perimeter for our unit which was plowing down jungles. We were not really infantry, we were combat engineers, trained to fight if necessary. But we had infantry that would guard us. This infantry unit would guard us day and night by setting up barbed wire perimeters, with claymore mines, guarding us with 2 ½ ton trucks with 4 mini guns and M50 in the center and soldiers guarding us 24 hours seven days a week. We were sent out in the field for anywhere between 4 to 6 weeks and then come in and stay for a couple of days or weeks and then go back out to another site. One time when we came into a base camp for a few weeks. Two of the men in the engineering company got into a fight with one of the 1st Cavalry infantry soldiers. It elevated so heavy they resorted to weapons and began shooting at one another. One man shot and killed the other. How can this happen? We are supposed to be in the same army. What a disgrace, what a discredit to unity. We were one man short because one thought themselves better than the other. That is disunity mixed with pride. *"Pride goeth before destruction, and an haughty spirit before a fall." (Proverbs 16:18 KJV)*. The church of Christ should not be fighting against one another. We are soldiers in the same military unit whether we be in the Army, Marines, Airforce, Navy, Coast Guard, or whatever branch of the armed forces. The same thing should go on with the Catholics, the Protestants, the Lutherans, the Methodists etc. We do not need to shoot our brothers. Satan and his dominions are our enemies, NOT one another. We are trying to please our Captain.

We who are followers of the Lord Jesus Christ should be so unified in our beliefs knowing that Christ is risen and those who say they believe in him should be working together with one another at the same goal of winning souls to Christ. Should not what binds us together in the life, the death, the resurrection, and Jesus second coming, be our motivating force for unity? We, the church must lay aside our petty differences that mean nothing to a person's eternal life and work toward the same goal of making disciples of Christ?

2 Timothy 2:3 & 4 NASB says "Suffer hardship with me, as a good soldier of Christ Jesus. No soldier in active service entangles himself in the affairs of everyday life, so that he may please the one who enlisted him as a soldier." We know from John 10:10 the devil comes to steal kill and destroy. Many Christian believers are also defeated in their walk with Christ by friendly fire. You have heard it in the news, some soldiers are wounded and even killed by friendly fire. Friendly fire can be accidental, but some are self-inflicted and done intentionally. I have heard that several soldiers in war times have shot themselves in the foot hoping they would be sent home. Some Christian soldiers shoot themselves in the foot by not standing firm on the Word of God and they cripple themselves. A slip of the tongue, or gossip could be accidental friendly fire but be careful and hold your tongue. Here are three things you can do with gossip. You can collect it for a rainy day to get back at your brother, you can scatter it openly anywhere you want to, or you can dispose it in a trash can where it belongs.

The spiritual gifts God gives you are supernatural to help you walk the path God has for you. Romans 11:29 tells us these gifts and your calling are irrevocable, meaning, God is not going to take back the gift He gave to you. That is a way of saying; do not bury these gifts in the sand. There are consequences. You may be demoted to private for not obeying orders. *Matthew 25:24-27 NASB says "And the one who had received the one talent came up and said 'Master, I knew you to be a hard man, reaping where you did not sow and gathering where you scattered no seed. And I was afraid and went away and hid your talent in the ground. See, you have what is yours, "But his master answered and said to him, 'You wicked, lazy slave, you knew that I reap where I did not sow and gather where I scattered no seed. Then you ought to have put my money in the bank, and on my arrival, I would have received my money back with interest."*

THREE PASSAGES OF SCRIPTURE INTRODUCE US 16 GIFTS OF THE HOLY SPIRIT. NINE ARE LISTED IN 1 CORINTHIANS 12:8-10 AND 7 MORE GIFTS ARE LISTED IN ROMANS 12:6-8

*1 Corinthians 12:8-10 ASV "For to one is given through the Spirit the **word of wisdom**; and to another the **word of knowledge**, according to the same Spirit: {9} to another **faith**, in the same Spirit; and to another **gifts of healings**, in the one Spirit; {10} and to another **workings of miracles**; and to another **prophecy**; and to another **discerning of spirits**: to another **divers kinds of tongues**; and to another the **interpretation of tongues:** {11} but all these worketh the one and the same Spirit, dividing to each one severally even as he will."*

<u>Three gifts are Revelatory Gifts:</u>

- The Word of Wisdom
- The Word of Knowledge
- The Discerning of spirits

Three gifts are Power Gifts:

- Faith
- Healing
- Miracles

Three gifts are Vocal Gifts:

- Prophesy
- Tongues
- Interpretation of Tongues

The other 7 Gifts listed in Romans 12:6-8:

- Giving
- Exhortation
- Teaching
- Leading
- Mercy
- Administration
- Helps

Let us look at these gifts a little closer.

REVELATORY GIFTS

1. **Gift of Wisdom**. It is the supernatural ability to apply both divine and human wisdom (1 Kings 3:16-17). King Solomon and the judgement he made about the baby, where the two

mothers were fighting saying this baby as theirs. The one baby had died during the night and the one mother switched the babies around, but the real mother knew it was her baby who lived. They took the case to the king. King Solomon had wisdom from God. Saying, "God show me who is the mother here?" Solomon told a soldier to get a sword, cut the baby in half, and give each mother a half. Obviously, the real mother would not allow her baby to be killed and immediately gave up the baby that the child may live. Of course, King Solomon recognized true love and had the baby given to the real mother. This kind of wisdom from God is what King Solomon prayed for and he received it through faith.

Another example is the deacon Phillip with the Ethiopian Eunuch when he went down to Gaza as the Holy Spirit led him, and he explained supernaturally because he was asked to interpret Isaiah. Philip did so by receiving revelation from God. (See Acts 8). For the soldier, the fear of the Lord is the beginning of Wisdom. God also says through *Isaiah 66:2 KJV "but to this man will I look, even to him that is poor and of a contrite spirit, and that trembleth at my word."*

As you can see, wisdom is understanding what to do with knowledge.

2. **Gift of Knowledge**. This is the supernatural ability to apply Divine and Human knowledge given you by God. Elisha knowing the Syrian king is planning to capture him for the reason that he knew the king's battle plan before he came against Israel summarizing there was a spy in his kingdom. The king of Syria was asking his prophets what was going on here, he said "I sent my soldiers to do this and that and is like the king of Israel knows what I am going to do before I do it." They replied to him that it was because the prophet Elisha's God tells

71

him what you are going to do while he is in his bedroom. (See 2 Kings 6:12). That is knowledge from God.

Again in 2 Kings 6:17, Elisha knows there are horses and chariots of fire surrounding the city of Dotham. Elisha's servant was scared to death because there was an army coming to capture or kill Elisha. However, Elisha prayed to the LORD and said, "open my servant's eyes." Elisha had that supernatural ability and divine knowledge to know that God's forces were much stronger, and that God's forces were surrounding the city.

Peter also had the knowledge of the Lord about Ananias and Sapphira, at the beginning of the church. This was knowledge given to Peter by the Lord. How would he know that they had withheld back a portion of the money? Only by revelatory knowledge from the Lord. (Acts 5).

Then there was Peter again when he was directed to the gentile centurion Cornelius's house. This was also the word of knowledge given to Peter by God.

Paul had the same gift when the ship broke up on his way to Rome, He told everybody to stay with the ship and you will be saved. He had that supernatural knowledge from the Lord. (Acts 27).

And likewise, the soldiers of Christ must keep in constant communication with God and hear his voice through his word. *"God, after He spoke long ago to the fathers in the prophets in many portions and in many ways, (2) in these last days has spoken to us in His Son, whom He appointed heir of all things, through whom also He made the world." {Hebrews 1:1 NASB}*

3. __Gift of Discerning of spirits__. This is the supernatural ability to distinguish between human, demonic and divine works. All the Old Testament false prophets lacked this gift. They would mix a little bit of truth with subtle lies, and they fooled a lot of people, but they did not fool Elijah at Mount Carmel, (1 Kings 18).

In the New Testament Peter had that gift when he discerned Simon who practiced sorcery and he rebuked that demonic spirit in Simon (Acts 8:9-23). Simon wanted to buy with money the supernatural ability to lay hands on people and then have them receive the baptism of the Holy Spirit.

Paul also was given discernment from God concerning Elymas {Bar-Jesus} in Acts 13:10, as he discerned that Elymas was trying to keep the governor from receiving Jesus. Paul rebuked him with these words. *"You who are full of all deceit and fraud, you son of the devil, you enemy of all righteousness, will you not cease to make crooked the straight ways of the Lord." (Acts 13:10 NASB)* This was discerning of spirits at work.

Paul again in Acts 16:16-24, knew the slave girl possessed the spirit of divination. Paul had the gift of discerning the spirits, and the revelatory gift of discerning of spirits came in useful again. He knew the difference between the evil from the truth, and that is supernaturally given by God.

GIFTS OF POWER:

1. __Gift of Faith__. Faith is the supernatural ability to believe in what we cannot see. *"Jesus answered saying to them, "have faith in God. "For verily I say unto you, That whosoever shall say unto this mountain, Be thou removed, and be thou cast into the sea; and shall not doubt in his heart, but shall believe that those things which he saith*

shall come to pass; he shall have whatsoever he saith. (24) Therefore, I say unto you, What things soever ye desire, when ye pray, believe that ye receive them, and ye shall have them." (Mark 11:22-24 KJV). "Faith is the assurance of things hoped for, the conviction of things not seen." (Hebrews 11:1 NASB).

There are three types of Faith, saving faith, sanctifying faith, and stewardship faith. We see **saving faith** when Naaman the Syrian general who was a leper, who went to Elisha to be cured of his leprosy, and Elisha sent him to the Jordan to wash seven times, although he was disappointed that Elisha would not see him, he went ahead and did it by faith and after dipping seven times in the Jordan River he was healed and proclaimed the *"God of Israel is God" (2 Kings 5:1-14)*. And he began sacrificing to Yahweh. He had saving faith at this point.

Likewise, in Acts 16:31 which is one of my favorite life verses, as God gave me that verse as a young believer, he said to me *"if you believe on the Lord Jesus Christ and you will be saved and your house."* This word came to me as a Rhema word from God and I believed it and many of my family members were saved as the years went by. Therefore, he who comes to God must believe that He is and that He exists, and that he rewards those who seek him. *"Faith comes by hearing and hearing by the word of God." (Romans 10:17 KJV)* This is step one, believing there is a God and then being able to understand who Christ is and what he has done for us at the cross.

Then we have **sanctifying faith**, which is available to all believers, in other words we have been set apart. Paul said it in *Galatians 2:20, "I have been crucified with Christ; and it is no longer I who live, but Christ lives in me; and the life which I now live in the flesh*

I live by faith in the Son of God, who loved me and gave Himself up for me."

The last is **stewardship faith**, which is a supernatural faith to believe and expect great things. Elijah was one such; he believed and knew God was going to answer him with fire. (1 Kings 18). Then Israel will know *"The Lord He is God"*. Stewardship faith never does anything for itself. Jesus never did anything for Himself with all the power He possessed. He used it for others. Romans 12:3 tells us that God has dealt to each one of us a measure of faith.

2. **Gift of Healing.** A supernatural ability to cure sickness in Jesus' name whether it is physical, mental or demonic in nature. We know that Isaiah 53:5-7 tells us by His stripes **we are healed**. This is repeated by Peter in 1 Peter 2:24 in the past tense, **we were healed**. A study of this passage will reveal to you his stripes bring healing to these three realms. An example from Scripture was the demoniac, the one that had the legion of demons. When Jesus healed him, he sat there fully dressed and completely in his right mind, the very man who had had the "legion" was now demon free. This man was healed physically, spiritually and delivered demonically all at the same time. The more I pray and study Scripture I see that God's nature is to heal. *"...He is the Lord who heals all our diseases."* A soldiers reasoning should be what is written in the following verses... *(Psalm 103:2-4 KJV). "Bless the LORD, O my soul, and forget not all his benefits: (3) Who forgiveth all thine iniquities; who healeth all thy diseases; (4) Who redeemeth thy life from destruction."* All believing soldiers by faith believe God forgives all our iniquities. They also believe that God delivers us from destruction. Then why cannot the soldiers of Christ understand and believe that God heals all our diseases? God is saying not to forget all His

benefits yet many believing soldiers of Christ forget the middle part of this verse… "HE HEALS ALL OUR DISEASES? Therefore, His very nature is healing. The LORD wants to heal you spiritually but of course sometimes he heals the flesh to get to spirit, and other times He heals the spirit and the flesh. You must remember this history lesson given to us by the Israelites exiting Egypt complaining in the wilderness. *Psalm 78:41 KJV "Yea, they turned back and tempted God, and limited the Holy One of Israel."* In other words, learn from Biblical history…**DO NOT LIMIT GOD.**

3. <u>**Gift of Miracles**</u>. The supernatural ability to perform activities beyond what supersedes the laws that we know. You saw that all through the Scriptures, that in the book of Genesis Moses parted the Red Sea. Do you know the Jordan River was parted three times? Joshua parted it when he went into the promised land of Canaan. Elijah parted it as he threw his mantel on the water of the Jordan River, and it opened allowing Elijah and Elisha to cross over to the other side. There the LORD took Elijah home in a chariot of fire. The mantel fell on Elisha, and he went back across the Jordan. Once again, the Jordan River was parted for the third time. These are supernatural miracles that God has done through these prophets.

In the New Testament, many miracles are performed by believing saints. Jesus heals the blind man who was blind at birth. Peter and John healed a lame man at the temple gate called "Beautiful" (Acts 3). We also see Paul raising Eutychus from the dead after falling from the third story window asleep as Paul preached late into the night. (Acts 20:8-12)

Miracles are a supernatural sign that demonstrates a spiritual truth; And that spiritual truth is that Jesus Christ is the Lord.

THREE GIFTS ARE VOCAL GIFTS:

1. **Gift of Prophecy**. It is the supernatural ability to obtain and communicate revelations from God. The Old Testament prophets would tell us what God was going to do in the future. Some of them were non-writing prophets and some of them were writing prophets. Therein is the reason they are called them Major and the Minor prophets. None are more or less important than the other. They all have prophetic insights to the future, yet they also give us historical information. We are also told in the Scriptures that the testimony of Jesus is the Spirit of prophesy. Preaching then is a form of prophecy and not necessarily about the future.

2. **Gift of Tongues**, is a sign for the believer not the unbeliever. It is a supernatural ability to have a communication with God that no one knows or understands, even the enemy. I can relate to this gift because I was a soldier, and I was taught how to send and receive Morse Code. I could send a message to another soldier in Morse Code and the enemy would have no idea of what I said. Tongues are a communication between you and God and that is why it is the least of the gifts because it edifies self. *"He that speaketh in an unknown tongue edifieth himself; but he that prophesieth edifieth the church. (1 Corinthians 14:4 KJV)* All the other gifts edify the body of Christ."The Devil has twisted this gift to confuse the church and that is why some people do not even want this gift. If this gift in not in operation in the church it will weaken the church. How... because the devils hear your battle plan and set up ambushes to take you out. The element of surprise is of great advantage to an army. You must remember it is the Spirit that gives the gifts and distributes them as He wills. *"But one and the same Spirit works all these things, distributing to each one individually just as He wills." (1 Corinthians 12:11 NASB)*

"These signs will accompany those who believe in my name, in my name they will cast out demons, they will speak with new tongues..." *(Mark 16:17 NASB).*

There are different manifestations of tongues. This is a study in itself. We will not dive into this but let us simply state this.

One is a "PRAYER LANGUAGE." This is direct communication with God through you which was given by the Holy Spirit who lives within you. There is no need for interpretation by you. God knows what is being said, after all it is His Spirit in you doing the praying when you do not know how to pray. *"For he that speaketh in an unknown tongue speaketh not unto men, but unto God: for no man understandeth him; howbeit in the spirit he speaketh mysteries."* *1 Corinthians 14:2 KJV*

Another is when God gives a message to others through you. The direction of communication is from God. This is a form of prophesy. There must be an interpretation if the message is in an unknown language. *1 Corinthians 14:27 KJV "If any man speak in an unknown tongue, let it be by two, or at the most by three, and that by course; and let one interpret. (28) But if there be no interpreter, let him keep silence in the church; and let him speak to himself, and to God.*

The third type of tongues is when God gives a message to people in THEIR native language which you do not know. It is a KNOWN language, often experienced by missionaries. Also seen in the Scriptures. *Acts 2:4-11 KJV "And they were all filled with the Holy Ghost, and began to speak with other tongues, as the Spirit gave them utterance. (5) And there were dwelling at Jerusalem Jews, devout men, out of every nation under heaven. (6) Now when this was noised abroad, the multitude came together, and were confounded, because that every man heard them speak in his own language. (7) And they were all amazed and marveled, saying one to another, Behold, are not all these which speak Galileans? (8) And how hear we every man in our own tongue, wherein we were born? (9) Parthians, and Medes, and Elamites, and the dwellers in Mesopotamia, and in Judaea, and Cappadocia, in Pontus, and Asia, (10) Phrygia, and Pamphylia, in Egypt, and in the parts of Libya about Cyrene, and strangers of Rome, Jews and proselytes, (11) Cretes and Arabians, we do hear them speak in our tongues the wonderful works of God."*

3. **Gift of Interpretation of Tongues.** The interpretation of tongues is the supernatural ability to interpret messages that are spoken in an unknown language. In the Old Testament, there is no such gift. In *1 Corinthians 13:10 "But when that which is perfect is come, then that which is in part shall be done away."* 1 Corinthians 13 is the love chapter. Have you noticed how the Lord has placed the love chapter in the Bible between the two chapters explaining the gifts of the Holy Spirit? I believe the Lord allowed this to be done purposely that men must know that love is necessary between fellow soldiers on these issues. It tells us that the gifts are valid until the perfect comes. Some say the perfect means the Bible. Some say the gifts ended when the last of the apostles died. Some believers deny that there is any such thing as a New Testament apostle. None of these ideas can be supported by proof, yet they are prevalent in both denominational and non-denominational Churches! The **Perfect** is the second coming of Jesus Christ who is **Perfect.** This would mean that the gifts are still in effect today because the Lord Jesus has not returned in His second advent. Many believers argue that some of the gifts are no longer in operation. Yet the Scriptures are clear *that... "Jesus is the same, yesterday, today, and forever."* They say that which is in part will be done away with, therefore, once Jesus comes back the **perfect** will appear on earth. Then

some of the gifts will be done away with being no longer necessary. Instead of praying to God, you will be seeing him face to face. Faith, hope and love will be the three that will remain when the **perfect** comes. *(See 1 Corinthians 13:13)*

THE NEXT SEVEN GIFTS ARE LISTED IN ROMANS 12:6-8 ESV.

Usually referred to as **Stewardship Gifts**. *"Having gifts that differ according to the grace given to us, let us use them: if prophesy, in proportion to our faith; (7) if service, in our **serving**; the one who teaches, in his **teaching**; (8) the one who exhorts, in his **exhortation**; the one who **contributes (helps)**, in **generosity (giving)**; the one who **leads**, with zeal; the one who does acts of **mercy**, with cheerfulness."*

- Giving
- Exhortation
- Serving (ministering)
- Teaching
- Leading (Administration)
- Mercy
- Helps

These Gifts are <u>Others Oriented</u> and Edify the Church of Christ.

1. <u>**Giving**</u> is the supernatural ability to give. Not just money or tithes, but also possessions, giving time and talent unto the Lord's work. *Exodus 36:2-5 NKJV, says "…Everyone whose heart was stirred to come and do the work for the temple. They received from Moses all the contributions which the sons of Israel had brought to perform the work in the construction of the temple. And they*

continued bringing to him freewill offerings every morning. And all the skillful men who were performing all the work of the temple came, each from the work which he was performing and said to Moses, 'The people are bringing much more than enough for the construction work which the Lord commanded us to perform."

These people are not just giving their time; they are giving their money and their talents as well to work on the temple. Therefore, giving is not just money. This world thinks it is run by money, but it is not. Yes, it's true, money is needed to fund the work that we do, but it's not all about money. It's about letting the Lord build the church. If we don't, we are laboring in vain. I have experienced businessmen whose businesses slow down, then they come and volunteer of their time. They give the church of their time and talents, doing all sorts of repairs here and there, plumbing, painting, carpentry etc. Then eventually they must go back to their work because God blesses their businesses. I know when they come, they won't be here long because every time the Lord rewards them. They would always finish what they started, but they would come and say… "Pastor Joe I did not want to disappoint you, but I have to go back to work." I would say to them, "You don't have to say a word, I already know exactly what happened, God has blessed your business so much that you must leave to attend to it." That is always what happens. God always gives back; you can never out give God.

2. <u>Exhortation</u> is the supernatural ability to encourage and challenge another believer. Jonathan did that with David. Jonathan, King Saul's son was in line to be king of Israel, but he encouraged David because he knew David was called to be king. Where would Paul be without Barnabas's exhortation and encouragement? He is the one who realized Paul was born again and now a follower of the Lord Jesus Christ. He removed the element

of fear from the original disciples of Christ, encouraging both Paul and the early church leadership. {Acts 11}

Then there is Judas, (not Iscariot) and Silas themselves being prophets exhorted and strengthen the brethren with many words. Some of us have the gift of exhortation / encouragement. *Acts 15:32-33 NKJV.* *"Now Judas (not Iscariot) and Silas, themselves being prophets also, exhorted and strengthened the brethren with many words. (33) And after they had stayed there for a time, they were sent back with greetings from the brethren to the apostles."*

3. We also have the **gift of teaching**, the supernatural ability to communicate or simplify or explain Bible passages. Ezra had the gift of teaching in the Old Testament and used it wisely when the Hebrews came back to Jerusalem after the 70 years of deportation to Babylon. When you see a teacher, you will see several gifts in action.

Aquila and Priscilla the New Testament saints were mighty in the Scriptures, and they taught accurately explaining them to Apollos. *{Acts 18:23-25}*

Therefore, the spiritual gift of teaching is a supernatural ability given by the Lord through the Holy Spirit to believers to apply these truths to our Christian walk.

4. Next, is the ability to **Lead.** Josiah in 2 Chronicles 34, was a young boy king. At age 8 he led Israel in the ways of the Lord.

In the New Testament <u>uneducated</u> men led better than people that were well educated. The scribes and the Pharisees realized that the young uneducated men had been with Jesus which is why they could lead the New Testament church. *Acts 4:13 KJV* *"Now when they saw the boldness of Peter and John, and perceived that they were unlearned and ignorant men, they marvelled; and they took* knowledge *of them, that they had been with Jesus."*

5. After that, we have the gift of **Mercy**, the supernatural ability to minister to the sick and the suffering, these people have a soft heart of compassion. Elijah, Elisha, and Jesus are examples of having compassion. Compassion is necessary and vital to be able to have an effective ministry to others.

6. **Administration** is the supernatural ability to organize and minister, manage or promote people or ventures. The rebuilding of the wall and the temple in Jerusalem was done by a man named Nehemiah and with his gift of administration he got the job done quickly against much opposition. Paul appointed Titus to use his gift of administration to set the church in order by appointing elders in every city. Titus and Nehemiah had the gift of Administration. Also, the deacons in Acts chapter 6, were full of the Holy Spirit and Wisdom, they had the gift to organize, being called to organize the feeding of the widows.

7. **The gift of helps** is the supernatural ability to give practical help both physically and spiritually. This gift always demonstrates agape love to those being helped.

    Ahimelech the priest helped David when he was in dire straits. David had no food to feed his men, he had no weapons, and Ahimelech gave him the sword that belong to Goliath that was wrapped in a cloth in the sanctuary; David had no idea it was there. It cost Ahimelech the priest his life because king Saul found out what he did and killed him for helping David escape.

Then consider Abigail who ended up being one of David's wives. She helped David when he needed to feed his men because her husband Nabal refused to give David food. David was about to wipe him out. Abigail came and prevented her husband from being killed by David as she was also helping David by feeding David and his men.

Phoebe in Romans 16 was a helper of many. When people do such things, they are helpers and are doing what the Lord wants to accomplish. We know from Matthew 25:40, that in doing this we are helping Jesus. When you feed the hungry, you are feeding Jesus, when you visit someone in jail, you are doing that to Jesus.

These things are very important to understand, however many people overlook them. You must remember that the Spirit Himself distributes the gifts to each one individually as he wills, it is not your will, it is the Holy Spirit's will. (See 1 Corinthians 12:11). Also remember, the purpose of the gifts is for the profit of all the church. (1 Corinthians 12:4-7)

If you have a "complaint" with these gifts, then you must take it up with the Holy Spirit of God for He distributes the gifts. Remember these gifts and the calling are irrevocable, (Romans 11:29) so he is not going to take our gifts away.

We also have the **spiritual offices** listed in *Ephesians 4:11 NASB*. *"He {God} Himself gives some as **apostles**, and some as **prophets**, and some as **evangelists**, and some as **pastors**, and **teachers**, for the equipping of the saints for the work of the ministry and for edifying the body."* God the Father would be likened to a five-star General, and Jesus of course is the Captain (usually the highest ranking field officer), and the Holy Spirit is the power operation on earth liken to the artillery used within an army strategy. A soldier's artillery is the Word of God. After all that's where the power lies. The apostles might be like lieutenants, the sent-out ones into the battle. The prophet might be ranked as a second lieutenant and the evangelist as a master sergeant. The top sergeant would be like the pastors because they are teachers. Although teachers are not always pastors.

A pastor is called to feed, nurture, protect and care for God's sheep. *"Jesus said to Simon Peter, "Simon, son of Jonah, do you (agape') love Me more than these?" He said to Him, "Yes, Lord; You know that I (phileō) love You." He said to him, "Feed My lambs." (16) He said to him again a second time, "Simon, son of Jonah, do you (agape') love Me?" He said to Him, "Yes, Lord; You know that I (phileō) love You." He said to him, "Tend My sheep." (17) He said to him the third time, "Simon, son of Jonah, do you (phileō) love Me?" Peter was grieved because He said to him the third time, "Do you (phileō) love Me?" And he said to Him, "Lord, You know all things; You know that I (phileō) love You." Jesus said to him, "Feed My sheep." (John 21:15-17 NKJV)* NOTICE: Jesus and Peter's play on the word LOVE. Jesus wants to know if Peter loves Him unconditionally {agape} and Peter is now humble knowing that his personal love for Jesus is not yet perfect love. After all Peter denied Jesus three times. Now, Peter is a humble man and can lead the sheep of God.

As you serve the Lord you are growing in the fervency of spirit, fervency in love, fervency in speaking truth, fervency in serving, and fervency in prayer. You are developing yourself as you go through basic training, and A.I.T. Usually when you complete your basic training, and A.I.T., (Advanced Instructional Training) you have your Military Occupational Specialty {MOS}, you will be receiving a promotion, for God sees your commitment to what He wants you to do. Remember Ittai the Gittite, who joined David's army the day before David was fleeing Jerusalem from his son Absalom. David told him to go home with his 600 men, but he would not. Do you know Ittai's response to David's words? Remember Ittai's response, it is IMPORTANT? *"as the Lord lives and as the lord my king lives surely and whatever place my lord the king shall be whether in death or in life, even there, also will your servant be."* David was impressed realizing he has a committed soldier and a future leader. This enlightened David that this man was committed to him and if he sent him to do something, he was going to get it done. What was David's response to his commitment? In *2 Samuel 18:1-2* *"David numbered the people who were with him and appointed over them commanders of thousands and commanders of hundreds. David sent out his troops, a third under the command of Joab, and a third under Joab's brother Abishai son of Zeruiah, and a* **third under Ittai the Gittite.** David had no worries about Ittai, he was committed to him, he was going to give his life if necessary, and when God sees devotion like that from His soldiers, believe me, God is going to promote you.

Luke 16:10 KJV tells us... *"He that is faithful in that which is least is faithful also in much: and he that is unjust in the least is unjust also in much."* David knew that Ittai was faithful in little, he had just joined the army 24 hours prior to Absalom's invasion. In 2 Samuel 23, you will also see that Ittai is listed as one of David's 37 mighty men. He was faithful; Ittai pleased his captain, his king and was promoted for it. David was impressed with him. Therefore, promotion follows absolute obedience.

IF YOU KNOW WHAT ARE YOUR SPIRITUAL GIFTS, THEN YOU MUST APPLY THEM AS YOU WALK IN FAITH.

"FORWARD MARCH"
"Becoming A Spiritual Christian Warrior Bringing Eternal Life to Men"

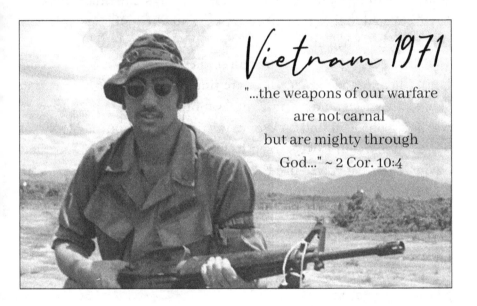

Vietnam 1971

"...the weapons of our warfare
are not carnal
but are mighty through
God..." ~ 2 Cor. 10:4

Chapter 5

A LIFE OF ACTIVE DUTY

Men and nations make war with damaging policies and strong words. Worldly armies fight with carnal weapons. The Christian soldiers fight with every Word of God, all 31,102 verses of Scripture are swords that you can use in holding up your shield of faith. The former does so to kill and take booty. The Christian soldier fights with the Sword of the Spirit the Word of God, to bring the peoples of the world eternal life through faith in Jesus Christ the LORD.

This chapter is concerning God's commission for the church to **"Forward March"** outside the stronghold of God's perimeter. What is a stronghold? The stronghold is a safe place. The church is the Christian soldier's stronghold. David retreated to his stronghold in times of trouble or to rest and regroup his army. Today's Christian churches have retreated to the stronghold some for hundreds of years. It is now time for the Christian churches to "FORWARD MARCH."

1 Samuel 22:1-5. For Christian soldiers, the church is the stronghold, where we all gather. There are times when we need to get outside of the stronghold because the "war of all ages" is raging. There is war going on all around us. We are warring against spiritual forces of wickedness trying to keep men from receiving Christ Jesus as their Savior. You are involved in a battlefield every day, like it or not. Some soldiers are effective, and some are still resting inside the church while men's souls are eternally at stake. Are we asleep in the church stronghold when we have been commissioned by our Captain Jesus Christ to "*Go therefore, and make disciples of all the nations, baptizing them into the name of the Father and of the Son and of the Holy Spirit? Matthew 28:19-20*

We were born into this battlefield. Satan has been warring in this battle for thousands and thousands of years. He is well versed in his strategy while we only have a few years in this battle. We need the Holy Spirit to show us these things. Have we forgotten that there is a multitude of people in the valley of decision? Many have not heard the good news of Jesus Christ. Being enlisted in the army of God you are being trained by the Holy Spirit. You have learned what gifts you have. Most likely you have been promoted to a higher rank by now. You have proven your loyalty to the Lord Jesus Christ. You are following in the footsteps of other soldiers who have gone before you who were absolutely committed to the Lord. My question is, ARE YOU?

Here are some of those soldiers:

- **David**: Psalm 146:1-2 says, *"I will serve God while I have my being"*.

- **Job**: in *Job 13:5 KJV "though he slay me, yet shall I serve him."*

- **Daniel**: went to the lion's den saying, *"I will not bow before Nebuchadnezzar."*

- **Shadrach, Meshach and Abednego** had a similar commitment. *"If it be so, our God whom we serve is able to deliver us from the burning fiery furnace, and he will deliver us out of thine hand, O king. {18} But if not, be it known unto thee, O king, that we will not serve thy gods, nor worship the golden image which thou hast set up." (Daniel 3:17-18 KJV).*

- **Moses** chose to suffer with the Jews, rather than enjoying pleasure for a season.

- In **Noah's** time it had never rained on earth when he built the ark. The earth's weather was tropical, so when he told the people rain was going to fall from the sky, they thought Noah was crazy and for 120 years the people laughed at him.

- **Paul**: *"for me to live is Christ and to die is gain"* (Philippians 1:21 KJV).

- **Stephen**: went about preaching the gospel as a church appointed deacon, exceeding his calling to wait tables for the women. He preached and was brutally martyred for it.

- **James**, the brother of John was killed by the sword. *(Acts Chapter 12).*

- **John Mark** deserted Paul and Barnabas during the first missionary journey. Yet in *2 Timothy 4:11,* Paul is calling for John Mark saying, *"he is useful to me."* John Mark had made an "about face" and he was now back into the soldier calling. John Mark of course is the one who wrote the Gospel of Mark.

Talk about commitment, these men were loyal and committed Christian soldiers of Christ.

We are following in the footsteps of these courageous faith filled soldiers.

The apostle Paul did a great deal of talking about being a soldier of Christ. (*2 Timothy 2:1-4* and *Ephesians 6:10-20).* Why would he not after being chained to them for several years?

All these soldiers were sold out or we could say "SOULED OUT" to the Lord. These men were not double minded. David was strikingly clear saying in prayer, *"give me an undivided heart, that I may fear your name." Psalm 86:11 NIV.*

As we become absolutely committed to the Lord. He will have some assignments for us. Thus, we cannot be double minded, you are either for Him or against Him. *"A double minded man is unstable in all his ways." (James 1:8 KJV)* Doubled minded here in Greek (dipsuchos) is referring to "doubled souled or even double spirited."

Now that we have been trained, it is time to "forward march" outside the perimeter. In every battlefield there are perimeters set up with barbed wire and guards all around. All soldiers are to stay inside the stronghold unless the captain give their orders shouting, **"Forward March."** Soldiers who proceed to go outside the perimeter without the orders from the Captain could end up either killed, wounded or captured.

These A.W.O.L. soldiers will figure out a way to climb over the barbed wire or crawl on their bellies to get to the battlefield without backup or accountability. This is how the Christian soldiers who venture outside of the ordinances of God slip and slide into the enemy's hands. Our Captain does send us outside the stronghold at times to do a work of ministry. The stronghold is also the place where we get equipped to fight in the battlefield. You must be strong and very courageous and then the Captain will send you out on a reconnaissance mission to redeem men through the preaching of the Word of God.

When we are ready, able and when He needs your trained specialty for the battle, he will order you on a special assignment to capture the souls of men by using the gift that you possess. In *1 Samuel 22 we see that "…David departed from there and escaped to the cave of Adullam, this is when Saul was chasing him, and he escaped to Adullam. When his brothers and all his father's household heard of it, they went down to him there and everyone who was in distress, or in debt or displaced gathered with him, and he became captain over them." About 400 men were with him, and David went from there to Mizpah in Moab and said to the king of Moab, 'please let my father and my mother come and stay with you until I know what God will do for me.' then he left them with the king of Moab, and they stayed with him all the time that David was in the stronghold. **But the prophet Gad said to David "do not stay in the stronghold, depart and go into the land of Judah"** so David left and went to the forest of Hereth."* Consequently, David retreated to the stronghold, the problem with that is, we believers and soldiers like to stay in the stronghold. It is safer there. But there is a time when we are called to go out. If you do not go you are disobeying the Captains orders and can be reprimanded. The prophet Gad was sent to David to tell him it was time to get out of the stronghold. God had anointed David to be king over Israel, it just had not been brought into fruition yet. Therefore, the church is the stronghold, but we cannot stay there forever. We have much work to do. The Lord has called us believers to preach the Good News. *"And Jesus came and spake unto them, saying, All power is given unto me in heaven and on earth. {19} Go ye therefore, and teach all nations, baptizing them in the name of the Father, and of the Son, and of the Holy Ghost: {20} Teaching them to observe all things whatsoever I have commanded you: and, lo, I am with you always, even unto the end of the world." (Matthew 28:18-20 KJV)*

The stronghold is where we are refreshed, encouraged, strengthened, equipped, re-energized, and revived. If we are forsaking the gathering of ourselves together, we will be at a great disadvantage. I am sure you've heard many believers say... "I don't need to go to church to be saved and to worship God. I can do that anywhere." They always try to justify themselves saying, I am a "Born Again" Christian and I do not want to hang out with a bunch of hypocrites? I will guarantee you that if you show me a Christian that thinks like this then I will show you a shallow and weak follower of Christ. Let me tell you again you need to be in the stronghold, but you are not to stay there. There is a time to go and a time to stay. There are a lot of good preachers on TV but that is not where you will have that one-on-one personal touch. Hence, there is a time for everything under the sun, there is a time to be in the stronghold and a time to be out of it.

2 Samuel 23, King David was at war with the Philistines and he was thirsty. Three of his men broke into the enemy camp and stole some water from the well of Bethlehem and brought it to David. When David found out how it was obtained, he would not drink it. He poured it out before the Lord and said... *"far be it from me Oh Lord that I should do this, is this not the blood of the men who went in jeopardy of their lives?"* In other words, these men went outside the stronghold without permission from David or God and in doing so, they put their very lives in danger. This was one of those times when you are not to go out of the stronghold. You will put yourself in danger and others with you. You only venture outside of the stronghold when God leads you. The prophet Gad had instructed David to do so, and he obeyed. As a result of this David became more well-known than ever. *"Everyone who was in distress or in debt or discontented gathered to him and he became captain over them."* God does not care where you come from, the color of your skin, nor your height, nor health, nor strength, nor if you are in debt, or how you are dressed. All he cares about is you.

Therefore, the soldier's mission for Christ is to go to the entire world and make disciples when God calls us out of the stronghold. We must all do our part. You see the devil thinks he is in control; the Scriptures say differently. The Psalmist says… *"the heavens even the heavens are the Lord's but the earth he has given to the children of men."* The soldier of Christ must follow the Lord's command and obey if the Lord orders you to venture outside the perimeter. When He commands this then it is time to "March Forward" into the harvest fields. Jesus said, *"the fields are white for harvest."* White here is meaning ready to reap the fruits of the laborers.

When God calls, it is time to march forward as a good soldier of Christ. The Spirit of God dwells in your heart and when the Spirit of God rises it is time to move. Compassion for the lost will be your motivating factor mirroring your Captain Jesus. This compassion for the lost is what drew Him outside the perimeter of the Kingdom of Heaven. You, like Jesus will realize there are people out there dying in their sins. Our battle is like our Captain's, the battle for the souls of men. Now, more than ever it is time to "Forward March."

Let us look at Paul and Barnabas as they were moving outside the stronghold, being led by the Holy Spirit. *Acts 13:1-4 KJV…* Paul was extremely active preaching in a local place being in the presence of several prophets. These prophets prophesied this… *"Now there were in the church that was at Antioch certain prophets and teachers; as Barnabas, and Simeon that was called Niger, and Lucius of Cyrene, and Manaen, which had been brought up with Herod the tetrarch, and Saul. {2} As they ministered to the Lord, and fasted, the Holy Ghost said, Separate me Barnabas and Saul for the work whereunto I have called them. {3} And when they had fasted and prayed, and laid their hands on them, they sent them away. {4} So they, being sent forth by the Holy Ghost, departed unto Seleucia; and from thence they sailed to Cyprus."* As a result, they were called out of the stronghold by the Holy Spirit. Paul and Barnabas then go out on their first missionary journey. This was their call to March Forward. Now their first reconnaissance mission is about to take place. Firefights are soon to follow as they venture forward from the stronghold in Antioch. They then march to the island of Crete, then Salamis, Paphos, Perga and the Pisidia Antioch which is on the northern border of the Mediterranean Sea. Then on to Iconium which is also in Pisidia, then Lystra where Paul was stoned to death but raised. Next Derbe, then back to Lystra and back to Iconium then back to Antioch and Perga, Pamphylia and then to Attalia. This is where the first mission ends and then they march back to the stronghold several years later, where they reported to the church at Antioch glorifying God.

During that mission Paul experienced great trials and tribulations, consequently it was not a joy ride. It was not for a wimpy soldier of Christ. Paul experienced all kinds of trials, they try to sacrifice to him because they thought he was some kind of god, they stoned him because the Jews followed him and caused all kinds of trouble, they took him outside of Lystra and stoned him to death. Paul is raised and goes back into Lystra and the next day he departs for Derbe and then preaches there for a while. Then goes straight away back to Lystra. At the end of that recon mission there were four churches started in the cities to which he and Barnabas visited. There was the Pisidia Antioch church, also in Iconium there was a church started, there were disciples in Lystra, and in the city of Derbe, there were disciples made as well. It all cost Paul his life at one point, but God raised him up. Paul and Barnabas were always being persecuted in some way or another. As you can see, Paul and Barnabas experienced great difficulties and tribulations outside the stronghold during their first reconnaissance mission. The harvest was starting to finally come in. Many stone hearts were being changed to hearts of compassion after being called by the Holy Spirit. Paul and Barnabas were met with all kinds of adversities but that did not stop them.

1 Chronicles 11:10-47. Tells us that in King David's time there were a few mighty men of God also who were fighting for God's kingdom to be established. One of them was Adino the Eznite, he loved his God and his king. He stood against 800 trained armed soldiers, and he won. There was no way Adino could stand against 800 men in the flesh, unless he had God's help. Mighty men do not run, they face impossible odds, but the victory is the Lord's.

Eleazer the son of Dodai the Ahohite , one of David's three mighty men had the Lord's help… " *when the Philistines who were gathered there to battle and the men of Israel had withdrawn." "He arose and struck the Philistines until his hand was weary and clung to the sword." 2 Samuel 23:10 NKJV.* The Lord brought about a great victory that day and he defeated the entire Philistine army by himself. He fought so hard that the sword was stuck to his hand." He did not lay down his sword. *"He who endures to the end will be saved." says the Scriptures. {Mark 13:13 NKJV; Matthew 24:13 NKJV}.* Let it be known, that if Eleazar had laid down his sword he would have certainly been killed but he did not. The parallel here is that the Christian soldier must never lay down the Word of God. It is this Sword of the Word of God that will cause the enemy to retreat.

"Now after him was Shammah the son of Agee a Hararite. And the Philistines were gathered into a troop where there was a plot of ground full of lentils, and the people fled from the Philistines." "But he took his stand in the midst of the plot, defended it and struck the Philistines; and the Lord brought about a great victory that day." He stood there all alone with his sword. (2 Samuel 23:11-12 NASB). Sometimes you will seem to be standing there all alone but do not worry the Lord is there with you. However, you have a responsibility to accurately handle the Sword of the Spirit which is the Word of God.

Abshai the brother of Joab, was another mighty man of King David. He lifted his spear against three hundred men and killed them. He was the most honored and became captain of the three mighty men. (See *2 Samuel 23:18)*

Benaiah the son of Jehoiada, who killed two lion like men who were five cubits tall on a snowy day. {Seven foot six inches}. (See *2 Samuel 23:20*).

All that to say that we are the mighty soldiers of God, and our Captain has already won the War of all the Ages. It has already been done. All the soldier of Christ must do is believe it and fight the little fire fights as we are on a reconnaissance mission until the Lord comes with all His myriads.

These passages show us there is a time to be still and time to 'Forward March." There is a time for everything under the sun. When a soldier of Christ is going through Basic Discipleship Training, he is given certain commands to obey. One of them is to "Right Face" at your Captain's orders. Then you will hear the words 'Foreword March' as you keep in step with every other trained soldier. Therefore, you are *"…not to forsake the assembling of ourselves together, as is the manner of some, but exhorting one another, and so much the more as you see the day approaching." (Hebrews 10:25 KJV)*. Remember, Inside the perimeter is where you go to be refreshed and encouraged by other believing soldiers of Christ. You will lose that blessing if you do not attend church. Where you worship, praise, grow in knowledge of Christ and fall in agape' love with Him and your brothers and sisters. The Lord's orders were to "Foreword March" with the responsibility to hold the ground you have just possessed in your Christian walk.

There was a soldier in the union army during the Civil War in the United States. His name was Brigadier General Joshua Chamberlain. He had orders to hold the hill called Little Round Top in Gettysburg Pennsylvania, being greatly outnumbered by the Southern Confederate Army. He obeyed his superior officers and with 300 men he held the hill according to his orders. These soldiers were very disciplined, they fought courageously and valiantly even though it seemed bleak because of the constant attacks and pressure put on from the southern confederate forces. He and his men held that ground obeying their orders. If they had not held that hill, it would have been sudden death to the

Union forces. These confederate soldiers would have broken through and flanked the Union army. And this would have changed the entire outcome of this Civil War. The application here is to hold the ground that you have taken back from the enemy during your Christian walk. In other words, do not back slide into your old ways. Your Captain is not pleased with the backsliders.

Today in the New Testament days we have become the mighty men of Jesus, we must remember He already won the war, it is already done. All we must do is win the battle. To win the battle you must come to know our enemies' weaknesses. For example, Goliath failed to recognize his enemy, all he saw was this little skinny young man. Goliath did not think about the God of this young man in front of him. Preachers today very rarely preach on this subject, about knowing the enemy. We should not be afraid of the enemy or demonic forces, they must get behind us, he is a defeated foe, you can remind him of this truth. The bottom line is we must know our enemy. We need to know he has a plan of destruction for every single one of us. Therefore, know your enemy and focus on his strategies, but do not be tempted to become preoccupied with him. Do not dwell on how strong he is because he has been stripped of his power. Dwell on the fact that Our Lord Jesus Christ has already rendered him powerless at the cross. *Ephesians 6:10–11* directs us to be strong and take our stand *"against the devil's schemes." "When He (Jesus) had disarmed the rulers and authorities, He made a public display of them, having triumphed over them through Him." (Colossians 2:15 NKJV)*. Since Scripture is interpreted by Scripture then the Word of God guarantees the devil has already been defeated.

Many believing soldiers have already been defeated because they do not believe the devil exists, even though Our Lord Jesus cast out demons several times and told us to do likewise. Demons who crippled people, demons that give people disease, demons that buckled them over, demons which made people throw themselves into the water to drown them and many more evil things. Every soldier of Christ must take warning that he is real. The devils job just keeps getting easier because you do not rebuke him in your Captain's Name. Then he gains more power from the others who do not challenge him, and they believe the same lie the devil told Eve and one by one he draws them in like a moth to the flame. Then they keep believing lie after lie until they sit in complacency and do nothing to counteract his deception. Soon after they believe just about anything. They even believe God is dead, and begin to dabble into astrology, horoscopes, witchcraft, and the like instead of running to our Savior. God Word means nothing to them. It just sits on the coffee table or on the bookshelf and no one reads it anymore as they forget what our Lord expects from His soldiers. The dust settles on the Bible and on their own hearts as they just open the door for the devil to enter.

This reminds me of another Captain. He was captured in a garden of Gethsemane and marched forward to take a hill called Calvary under the orders from his superior officer, the LORD God His Father. This Captain's soldiers deserted him and left him to fight this battle by Himself. The enemy pressed in and beat Him, insulted Him, humiliated Him and this Captain wondered why He had been abandoned. After prolonged agony He was executed being (K.I.A.) Killed In Action. It looked bleak as if the enemy won but when this Captain took his last breath this enemy was crushed instead of Captain Jesus being defeated. The enemy's fangs were smashed to powder and his claws were torn out. Satan therefore has been rendered clawless and toothless with a bruised head. Jesus Christ defeated the enemy who had the power of death **defeating death by, His death**. Since Jesus was sinless the penalty of death had no dominion over Him and He was resurrected from the dead just as the Scriptures say. The entire world past, present, and future was changed, and every man was given the ability to join Captain Jesus' ranks. Due to Christ's work at the hill called Calvary every Christian soldier has the power in Christ to run against a troop of our enemies since the enemy of God the devil has been defeated.

This Captain who was nailed to a cross on a hill called Calvary was not just an ordinary man. You must know and be certain that he was the one and only Son of the living God. When Captain Jesus conquered this hill, the sky grew dark, lightning flashed from East to West from North to South. As His blood ran down upon the cross to the earth, the earth quaked in mourning. When he drew his last breath and gave up His Spirit all of creation lamented. Genesis tells us when Abel's blood flowed to the earth it cried out to God. The Scriptures tell us that life is in the blood and as a result the very blood of Jesus cried out from the ground to God and the Earth was in deep mourning. The Creator who had created it had been K. I. A. Killed In Action. Can you imagine the scene in heaven? Was heaven silent? Was there rejoicing because the creator and King had returned to his throne? I really don't know at this point probably both. I am sad at this, yet I am also glad because *"For he hath made him to be sin for us, who knew no sin; that we might be made the righteousness of God in him."* {2 Corinthians 5:21 KJV}. It was my freedom, my redemption my victory which was purchased there. The enemy now is a defeated foe, and the soldiers of God are now free. I have chosen to give my life and allegiance to the Captain of the Host of the Armies of the Lord. I will March Forward in his name and repossess what the enemy is trying to steal from men, their very souls. The soldiers of Christ must not allow this to happen. There are billions of people waiting to hear the message you carry.

> *"Put in the sickle, for the harvest is ripe.*
> *Come, tread, for the wine press is full;*
> *The vats overflow, for their wickedness is great.*
> *(14) Multitudes, multitudes in the valley of decision!*
> *For the day of the LORD is near in the valley of decision."*
> *(Joel 3:13-14 NASB)*

Our Captain's will for His soldiers thus far is to... **#1 "ENLIST in God's Army", #2. "RE-UP", #3. "ABOUT FACE", and #4 "FORWARD MARCH"** into the battlefield in the name of Our Lord Jesus Christ with the sword of His Spirit which is the Word of God.

THE ENEMY HAS MANY TACTICS.

When the soldier is called outside the stronghold there are many dangers that he needs to be aware of. Outside the perimeter the soldier must always be watchful. Remember Gideon when he was called by the Angel of the LORD as a mighty man of valor? The Angel of the LORD told Gideon to go to battle against the Midianites. about 32,000 soldiers were willing to go to the battle. God said that was too many men otherwise Israel would think they had done it by their power. (See Judges 7:2-7). Whoever was fearful was sent home and as a result 22,000 departed and 10,000 remained with Gideon. These 10,000 were sent to the brook and only those who lapped the water with their hands were chosen for the battle. Did you ever wonder why these 300 remained? I'll tell you; it was because these 300 were always watching for their enemies as they drank, and they were always on the lookout for enemy attacks. So must the soldier of Christ always be ready for the attacks of the enemy. The devils love to catch the soldiers of Christ off their guard to wipe them out and make them ineffective soldiers.

These soldiers were always ready always looking and they are not about to get caught off guard by their enemy when they are called outside the perimeter by their Captain to take back what the enemy has stolen or to take new ground. These soldiers are always on the alert, strong, standing firm in their faith. They are not about to give up. A good soldier must always <u>watch, always be ready and always be faithful to his Captain.</u>

Booby-Traps:

The enemy has many booby-traps. Booby-traps are something you come upon unexpectedly. A good example might be when a man walks into a men's room and sees things that he didn't want to see. Such as an X-rated magazine, and/or evil words written on a bathroom stall. When he's driving down this highway and there's that X-rated billboard.

Tuning the TV channel seeing things you don't want to see. We are caught off guard unexpectedly. The enemy sets these booby-traps all around us. The soldier of Christ also must set booby-traps against the enemy. I know men and women who plant gospel literature, tracks, and the like in places where people will read. Giving your testimony of how you came to know Christ is a booby trap to the enemy because he is 99% sure you are not going to give it. When you do, it is a booby-trap to the enemy. A curve ball that he must counteract in some way. Your very words can bring eternal life to those who hear. These are all booby traps, that you can plant against the enemy. *"So shall my word be that goeth forth out of my mouth: it shall not return unto me void, but it shall accomplish that which I please, and it shall prosper in the thing whereto I sent it." (Isaiah 55:11 KJV).* Also remember the Lord fights with you… See *(Psalm 7:15-17 KJV). "But in the traps, they set for others, they themselves get caught. (16) So they are punished by their own evil and are hurt by their own violence. (17) I thank the LORD for his justice;"*

Claymore Mines:

What is a Claymore mine? Claymore mines are remote detonated directional mines firing large metal balls in a shotgun pattern. These claymores were set around the perimeter of a firebase or what we have called thus far the Christian stronghold. When the enemy attacks these claymore mines are set off remotely by a soldier. The soldier of Christ must be careful to know his enemy and what he might try to do. We need to study our enemy and because we have, we also will know some of his battle strategies.

In jungle warfare we were trained to know our enemy and let me tell you it is a jungle out there. We knew he had a habit of sneaking up during the night before the attack and turning these directional claymore mines around 180 degrees. In that way when we set them off, we would be killing ourselves. The soldier must be careful he is not outwitted by his enemy. Planting gospel literature, tracks and giving your testimony is as though you turned the claymore mines around on the enemy. Jesus told us that we must be wise as serpents yet harmless as a dove. Therefore, the soldier of Christ must use wisdom in his warfare and know his enemies battle strategies. *"Lest Satan should get an advantage of us: for we are not ignorant of his devices." (2 Corinthians 2:11 KJV).*

Joshua used a similar strategy when he marched against the city of Ai for the second time. See Joshua Chapter 8. The first time Joshua marched against Ai he sent only 3,000 men, {See *Joshua 7:3}.* The city was small, he failed to seek God on this decision. His men were defeated, and 36 men were lost. The men of the city of Ai chased Joshua's men outside the city walls. When Joshua found out what had happened, he went before the Lord, tore his clothes, fell on his face, put dust all over his head and cried out to the Lord. Joshua failed to go to the Lord for his battle strategy. When he did go before the Lord, after the guilty parties were dealt with God gave Joshua permission to march against Ai and promised that he would bring him victory. God told Joshua how to go about it. From the first attack Joshua knew what the men of the city would do. Therefore, he sent around the backside of the city a troop of men. He also sent troops to both sides of the front city gates. Then he attacked the city in the same way as the first attack. Joshua knew that the men of the city would chase his men outside the gates. Then Joshua had his men retreat just as before. Only this time the men of Ai would be flanked from the sides, as the men of Ai exited the city to attack Israel again. Joshua's troops flanked them on all four sides. The troops in the rear of the city then moved in and slaughtered those within as directed by the LORD God of Israel. The men of Ai were defeated. Why? Because Joshua new what his enemy would do. This is an example of how important it is to know your enemy.

Enemy Spies:

Enemy spies can be in the camp. We know that there was an enemy spy in Jesus's camp who betrayed Jesus. There were two spies sent into

Jericho to spy out the city. They were almost caught, but a women named Rahab was converted to the God of the Hebrews saying the God of Israel is God. For she had heard how the LORD God had parted the Red Sea and decimated the armies coming against Israel. She protected these spies as they were being sought by the king of Jericho. She was now a spy for Israel. Let me give you a parallel. There was a firebase in Southeast Asia, a small one just outside a large Air Force base. The small army camp had its Colonel who commanded the units stationed there. Every day South Vietnamese men and women were permitted to enter the base to do much needed work for which they were paid. The Colonel had a Vietnamese barber who shaved him regularly. This man had a straight edge razor in his hand while cutting his hair and shaving the colonel. I was told that one night there was an attack on the firebase. After the attack, soldiers went out to pick up the dead. The Colonel's barber was found to be among the dead. He could have slit the Colonel's throat at any time. He was a spy in our camp to gather information and to make a living to support his family. Christian soldiers of Christ you must be aware of spies in your camp. Therefore, you will not find any Scripture to tell you to take off your battle gear. The righteous armor of God must be always worn as it is protection. The helmet of salvation to protect your head from enemy mindsets, your eyes from lusts, etc. The breastplate of righteousness, which is Jesus Christ protects our vital organs, the belt of truth keeps us as honorable men in favor with God and man, the shoes protect our feet from detrimental debris. The shield of faith {God's Word} protects us from flaming arrows from the devil that may pierce our armor and do us harm. Lastly, the Sword of the Spirit which is the Word of God will slay the very spy that comes against us. If you are not wearing your armor and do not have the Word of God in your hand, then the enemy will ambush you and bring you harm.

Enemy Snipers:

These snipers are all around you ready to pick you off. You must be aware of their presence and not fall to their strategies leading you into sin. Snipers must be watched for when you are outside the stronghold of God. Man's heart is deceitful and desperately wicked. We must be careful and be on guard always. There is no room for you to think you are invulnerable. This complacency can destroy your witness for Christ. Therefore, stay focused and keep your glasses on for all soldiers have been given discernment from your Captain.

SPECIAL EQUIPMENT NECESSARY FOR EACH SOLDIER

Eyeglasses:

Some soldiers have been given special equipment. Eyeglasses are such a one. Many soldiers enter the Army, yet their eye site is poor. I know one soldier who refused to wear eyeglasses. He thought his site was good enough. One day as he was in a convoy, he was told to watch out as there are many snipers on this road. This soldier looked at the tree line and the coastline. As he looked at the trees which were quite a distance off, he noticed that they were blurry. He wondered how he could enhance his vision to see that far away. He remembered that he was issued eyeglasses, but they were geeky looking, and he would not wear them. Who cares he thought, I will try them on, and he placed them on his face? He then looked to the blurry tree line which was now clear, and he could see the green leaves of the trees. I know that soldier and he still wears eyeglasses to this day 50 years later. God has given us his Word that allows us to clearly see the world and all that is in it. We see the lies the enemy gives. We see the truth God has shown us. All soldiers of Christ are able to see clearly as he reads God's Word.

Camouflage:

Another of the specialized equipment is a camouflaged uniform. Camouflage uniforms help hide us from the enemy in whatever surroundings you may be. God says, *"because you have been my help, therefore in the shadow of your wings I will rejoice."* *Psalm 63:7 KJV.* God hides us in his shadow where it is hard for the enemy to see us. *"He who dwells in the secret place of the Most High shall abide under the shadow of the Almighty." (Psalm 91:1 KJV).* Therefore, if you DWELL and ABIDE in the LORD, you are hidden in God's shadow and are protected.

One day a man was walking his puppies. It was after dark. He had two puppies on a leash. As he walked around the corner of the house the motion censored spotlights came on, and when he looked for his puppies, they were nowhere to be found. He thought his puppies got off the leash somehow. He was frightened for a moment as he loved his puppies. Then he noticed the two puppies walking outside of the shadow that he was casting upon the yard where they were residing. They were hidden in the shadow of their master. Likewise, the soldier of God is camouflaged in his Master's shadow. God promises... *Psalm 91:3-4 KJV "Surely he shall deliver thee from the snare of the fowler, and from the noisome pestilence. {4} He shall cover thee with his feathers, and under his wings shalt thou trust: his truth shall be thy shield and buckler."* You are therefore hidden in the shadow of your Savior. *Colossians 3:3 KJV Verifies this... "For you died, and your life has been hidden with Christ in God. "*

Morse Code:

Morse Code was developed as a secret language using dots and dashes for every letter or numeral. It may not be specialized equipment, but special equipment is used for specialized communication. Therefore, Morse Code is a language that your enemy does not understand. When Morris Code is sent you are speaking to your allies. You are giving them information and / or requesting supplies and whatever else is necessary to win the battle. This specialized language that the enemy does not understand, I would compare this to the gift of tongues given to some believers by the Holy Spirit as written in Scripture in *1 Corinthians 12:11-12...."to another the working of miracles, to another prophecy, to another discerning of spirits, **to another different kinds of tongues,** to another the interpretation of tongues. (11) But one and the same Spirit works all these things, **distributing to each one individually as He wills."***

God has given some soldiers the ability to understand these dots and dashes to spell out valuable information necessary to bring victory. An example would be the Windtalkers of World War 2 who used an unknown Navajo Indian Language which Germans and Japanese armies did not know or understand. In the Army there are communication brigades also called signal units. These units set up radios and other forms of communication enabling one unit to talk with the next to coordinate their strategies. I was trained in Morse code. I was taught how to send and receive 15 five letter words per minute, 75 letters in 1 minute. Everyone in the military is not trained in this line of communication it is only for those who have been called to a signal unit. May I quote the above verse again? This is extremely important in Spiritual Warfare just as it is in carnal warfare...*1 Corinthians 12:11 NASB says '...but one and the same spirit works all of these things distributing to each one individually as He wills."* Morse Code is not understood by the enemy neither is the gift of tongues understood by the devil and his cohorts of darkness. Here is more Scripture... *"For he that speaketh in an unknown tongue speaketh not unto men, but unto God: for no man understandeth him; howbeit in the spirit he speaketh mysteries." (1 Corinthians 14:2 KJV).* Only those who have been skilled in communication must receive this training, therefore the Army called certain people who were gifted in this capacity. Many other soldiers are trained for different types of warfare, this is important in warfare and specialized communication.

THINGS A SOLDIER MUST AVOID AS HE MARCHES FORWARD

He Must Avoid Friendly Fire! Disunity is a huge part of the enemy's strategy to defeat the Christian soldier from within its own ranks. Jesus said… *"Every kingdom divided against itself is brought to desolation, and a house divided against a house falls, (18) If Satan also is divided against himself, how will his kingdom stand? Because you say I cast out demons by Beelzebub. (Luke 11:17-18 NKJV).* I call this Friendly Fire. Friendly fire is sometimes deliberate and sometime just lack of knowledge. Friendly fire can be many things, one such form is pride. My job is more important than yours. No, that is not true. We are all needed to fight in any battle. The enemy loves it when he causes disunity because instead of fighting him, we end up fighting ourselves. The soldiers of Christ must be unified in all things to be completely victorious otherwise a great fall will result. *"Pride goes before destruction, and a haughty spirit before a fall" (Proverbs 16:18 NKJV)* None of us are better than another. God loves us all the same and every soldier and his M.O.S. (Military Occupational Specialty) is of foremost importance in this spiritual battlefield. Pleasing our Captain should be a soldier's first and foremost motive. *"Suffer hardship with me, as a good soldier of Christ Jesus. (4) No soldier in active service entangles himself in the affairs of everyday life, so that he may please the one who enlisted him as a soldier." (2 Timothy 2:3-4 NASB).*

The Christian Warrior Must Avoid Being Drawn Outside the Perimeter Through Temptation

"But every man is tempted, when he is drawn away of his own lust, and enticed. {15} Then when lust hath conceived, it bringeth forth sin: and sin, when it is finished, bringeth forth death." (James 1: 14 – 15 KJV).

Some soldiers desire to live outside the parameters that God has set. They want to do it their way. If you, do it your way, you will soon find out that you will desire to sin. Sin will then fascinate you, and finally sin will assassinate you. Jesus told us to crucify the flesh. He said *'to take up your cross daily and follow Me."* That is if you wish to follow Him. It's true the word of God tells us that *"the payment for our sin is death but the gift of God is eternal life through Jesus Christ our Lord."* Living outside the perimeter can cost you extensively. Eskimos figured out how to get rid of pesty wolves that would steal their food. They would bury the handle of a razor-sharp knife in the ice. Then they would take a hunk of food and place it on the razor-sharp dagger. The hunk of flesh would be frozen solid. The wolves would come around to eat the flesh, but it was frozen like a popsicle on a stick. As they began to lick on the frozen meat the razor-sharp knife would begin to slightly filet their tongue. They would go into a feeding frenzy once they smell the blood, not realizing it was their own blood. As they begin to lick the meat, their tongues become lacerated to the point of losing so much blood that they will die. Sin is like that to mankind as we dillydally outside the perimeter of God, we find ourselves to be enticed by sin then we become fascinated by it and enjoying sin so much that we eventually find ourselves dead in our sins and rendered useless to God. *"Brethren, if any of you do err from the truth, and one convert him; {20} Let him know, that he which converts the sinner from the error of his way shall save a soul from death and shall hide a multitude of sins."* {James 5:19-20 KJV).

This can happen to you if you do not repent and return to the Lord escaping the snare of the devil. You are being held captive by him. Pray and be released from hid snare / booby-trap. *"And the servant of the Lord must not strive; but be gentle unto all men, apt to teach, patient, {25} In meekness instructing those that oppose themselves; if **God peradventure will give them repentance** to the acknowledging of the truth; {26} **And that they may recover themselves out of the snare of the devil, who are taken captive by him at his will."** (2 Timothy 2:24-26 KJV).

The Soldier of Christ Must Avoid Capture at all costs.

Outside the perimeter of God, a soldier can be captured. A soldier is to avoid capture at all costs. *Isaiah 59:19* tells us;" *When the enemy comes in like a flood, the Spirit of the Lord will lift up a standard against him.*" Did you know that Old Testament Scripture has no punctuation? I believe this verse can read very different from our perception. If we would take the comma **(,)** up above, after the word flood and place it where I believe it should belong. Which is after the word "in". Then this Scripture would read this way. *"When the enemy comes in,* ___*like a flood the Spirit of the Lord will lift up a standard against him.*___*" Is it really the enemy who comes in like a flood or is it God coming in like a flood and raising up a standard against our enemy."* **I BELIEVE IT IS GOD COMING IN LIKE A FLOOD.** When all seems bleak always know there is no surrender for the soldier of Christ. *(1 Corinthians 10:13 NASB)* says it this way, *"No temptation has overtaken you but such as is common to man; and God is faithful, who will not allow you to be tempted beyond what you are able, but with the temptation will provide the way of escape also, so that you will be able to endure it."*

Therefore, the soldiers of Christ must work together. There should be no friendly fire in the army of God. A kingdom divided against itself cannot stand and if a kingdom cannot stand it is the failure of its army.

"GUARD DUTY"
"Becoming a Watchful Christian Soldier."

Chapter 6

BEING ALERT AND READY
AT ALL TIMES

Guard duty is about protecting, feeding, and serving the sheep. There are a few things we must guard before we guard the Father's sheep that are under our care and management. Each one of us has a sheep under us, it could be your children, your grandchildren, or employees. A pastor may have many more, but there are always things that every one of us as a soldier must guard, and the most important one out of eight points is this.

1. Guard your heart.

*"Above all else, **guard your heart**, for everything you do flows from it."* Therefore, we must keep our hearts safeguarded. The New King James says to, *"keep your heart with all diligence for out of it springs the issues of life." (Proverbs 4:23 NKJV).* Thus, we as soldiers of Christ must guard our own heart. We also have a breastplate of righteousness issued to us which is the Lord Jesus Christ. As long as we keep it on, our heart will be protected. As a result, if we do not guard our heart, we will not be good to anyone. I would compare your heart with the Ark of the Covenant in the Old Testament. The Ark of the Covenant was designed by God. Moses wrote the instructions down in books of the law. The Ark was placed into the part of the Tabernacle called the Holy of Holies. Inside of the Ark of the Covenant were three items. *(Hebrews 9:4 / 1 Kings 8:9).* First was Aaron's staff which budded whenever the people rebelled against Moses and Aaron, concerning the spiritual leadership of the nation. There was also a golden jar of manna, which was angel food to sustain Israel as they traveled through the wilderness. It was their bread of life. Also contained within it was the second set of the Ten Commandment Tablets. The first set was destroyed when Moses threw them down and they were broken into pieces because he discovered the Israelites had made a golden calf to be their God. These tablets represent the Word of God. The three things in the Ark represented life, death and the bread of life and the incredible Word of God.

The priests carried the Ark as Moses commanded. We are also kings and priest according to the Scriptures described in *(Revelation 1:5-6 NASB)*. *"To Him who loves us and released us from our sins by His blood— (6) and He has made us to be a kingdom, priests to His God and Father."*

Therefore, we are kings and priests and each of us carries the Ark within us. The present-day Ark is where the Holy Spirit resides, and that place is in our hearts. Everyone who has asked Jesus Christ to come into his heart (with all his heart) has the Holy Spirit within him. Israel was commanded to follow the Ark, and we also are to follow the Ark, as our hearts containing the Holy Spirit leads us. Your heart is the Ark, where the presence of God dwells in New Covenant days. The Ark of the Covenant was where the presence of God dwelled in the Old Testament days also, and every time the presence of God moved then Israel packed up and moved. Same today when the presence of the Ark moves then we are to follow. That is what an Ark does, it follows.

The Ark of the Covenant was situated in the center of the camp heavily guarded by the Israelites. Likewise, the heart of man is the center of man and is to be heavily guarded. When the Ark came to rest, the Israelites would rebuild the tabernacle in the wilderness. The camp was set up in this way. On the right of the tabernacle the east side were three tribes, Judah was one of those tribes. On the north side three tribes, on the west side were another three tribes and on the south side there were also three tribes. Such that, when viewed from above, it forms a cross.

The parallel here is that our whole man, our spirit, soul, and body must also protect our heart. We know according to *(John 2:18-20 KJV) Jesus said… "destroy this temple, and in three days I will raise it up."* These are spiritual words, and the Jews could not understand them. They were always thinking and speaking carnally. They questioned the statement of raising the temple in three days since it took 46 years to build it. Jesus was not talking about a literal temple; He was talking about a spiritual temple. We also know that *1 Corinthians 3:16 and 6:19 NASB* tells us that… *"we are the temple of the Holy Spirit."* Remember the Holy Spirit lives within our hearts. We are now the temple of God. King Solomon built the temple to the plans David had made as the LORD dictated it to him. King David was not allowed to build it because he was a man of blood. The Ark of the Covenant was placed into the temple Solomon had built. The temple had three courts; the Holy of Holies where the Ark was placed, the Holy place where daily sacrificing was made, and the Outer Court where the Gentiles could find the Living God. This is why Jesus was zealous and said… *"you made my father's house a den of thieves."* They had set up the outer court with money changers and they were ripping people off. That was not the intention of God for the Outer Court; it was to be a place of prayer and a place where people could go to find and receive Yahweh as their Savior. We are now in the New Testament, and we have become the temple of the Holy Spirit and this whole temple should be saturated with the Holy Spirit of God.

Your heart {the Ark} can be captured by other things, which is what this chapter is about "guarding your heart." The Ark had been captured many times in Israel's history. And likewise, so can your heart be captured by things of this world. *(See 1 Samuel 4:1-11)*. When the Ark of God was captured, during the time of the Prophet Eli. The Word of God tells us that the glory had departed from Israel. When he heard this, Eli died as did his two sons Hophni and Phinehas. These fellows were priests in Israel, yet the Bible tells us they were wicked men and did not know the LORD. See *1 Samuel 2:22. "Now Eli was very old and heard all that his sons did unto all Israel; and how they lay with the women that assembled at the door of the tabernacle of the congregation."* Our hearts can get captured by this world and we must be very careful. *1 John 2:15-16 NASB, "Do not love the world nor the things in the world. If anyone loves the world, the love of the Father is not in him. (16) For all that is in the world, the lust of the flesh and the lust of the eyes and the boastful pride of life, is not from the Father, but is from the world."* These three things are killers, and Satan used them in the Garden of Eden to deceive Eve. It was part of Satan's plan, and therefore we need to watch for those deceptions, otherwise your heart can get captured by this world. When the Ark was captured in *1 Samuel 4:19-21*, Eli's daughter-in-law, the wife of Phinehas, was pregnant and near the time of delivery. When she heard the news that the ark of God had been captured and that her father-in-law and her husband were dead, she went into labor and gave birth, but was overcome by her labor pains. As she was dying, the women attending her said, "Don't despair; you have given birth to a son." But she did not respond or pay any attention. She named the boy **Ichabod**, because this name means, **"The Glory has departed"**—because of the capture of the ark of God and the deaths of her father-in-law and her husband."

THE APPLICATION: If your heart is not completely God's then the Glory of God, the Holy Spirit may not be present. We are told in 2 Corinthians 13:5 NKJV that we must, *"Examine yourselves as to whether you are in the faith. Test yourselves. Do you not know yourselves, that Jesus Christ is in you?—unless indeed you are disqualified. But I trust that you will know that you are not disqualified."* Therefore, repent of your sins and *"...if thou shalt confess with thy mouth the Lord Jesus, and shalt believe in thine heart that God hath raised him from the dead, thou shalt be saved. {10} For with the heart man believeth unto righteousness; and with the mouth confession is made unto salvation."* (Romans 10:9 & 10 KJV). Paul also tells us in *2 Corinthians 7:9-10 NKJV, "Now I rejoice, not that you were made sorry, **but that your sorrow led to repentance.** For you were made sorry in a godly manner, that you might suffer loss from us in nothing. {10} For godly sorrow produces repentance leading to salvation, not to be regretted; but the sorrow of the world produces death."* If you do not confess Him before men leading to repentance {making an About Face}, then how can He be in your heart? *Jesus said, "Behold, I stand at the door, and knock: if any man hear my voice, and open the door, I will come into him, and will sup with him, and he with me."* (Revelation 3:20 KJV). This tells you that Jesus is knocking at the door of your heart, but **you must invite Him in.** From then on you must "guard your heart" and stay in agape' love with Jesus. Hopefully, you have in the past opened your heart and invited Christ into your life. If you have not you must do it now. For today can be your day of salvation.

2. Guard your mind: *"And the peace of God, which surpasses all understanding, will guard your hearts and your minds in Christ Jesus." (Philippians 4:7 NKJV) "And do not be conformed to this world but be ye transformed by the renewing of your mind." (Romans 12:2 KJV)* "Therefore, guard your mind." You know the old computer cliché: garbage in garbage out, you put garbage in your mind and garbage will come out, you put good things in, and good things will come out. *Titus 3:5 NKJV says... "He saved us, not on the basis of deeds which we have done in righteousness, but according to His mercy, by the washing of regeneration and renewing by the Holy Spirit." This is exactly what we are talking about... guarding and renewing our minds. Sometimes we have worldly mindsets that need to go.*

3. Guard your soul: *Proverbs 22:5 NKJV "Thorns and snares are in the way of the perverse;*

He who guards his soul will be far from them." We must guard our mind, our heart and our soul which is the triune being that we are because we are made in the image of God. *"Abstain from all appearance of evil. Now may the God of peace Himself sanctify you completely; and **may your whole spirit, soul, and body** be preserved blameless at the coming of our Lord Jesus Christ." 1 Thessalonians 5:22–23 NKJV*

4. Guard yourself from the evil one: As the soldier of Christ, you must know your enemy. You must know where his resources, communications, and where his strong outposts are located. You must know what kind of weaponry he has and their locations. In 2001 the USA went to war against Afghanistan after their attacking of the twin towers in New York. The United States did not attack right away. Do you know what the U S government was doing first? They were studying their enemy, and when they found out where the communications, the artillery, the airfields were, then they struck full force and put the enemy in confusion. The USA knew their enemy's critical military positions. Do not dwell on how strong the enemy is but know your enemy and put him in a bad position. Dwelling on how strong he is, only takes your focus away from God. In *2 Thessalonians 3:3 NASB we read, "but the Lord is faithful, and He will strengthen and protect you from the evil one."* Jesus placed within the model prayer that we should *"pray that we be delivered from the evil one."* Yet when I hear people pray, they seldom mention *"God protect me from the evil one." Psalm 73:26 NASB "my flesh and my heart may fail, But God is the strength of my heart and my portion forever."* It is God who gives us the victory over the devil. The devil was defeated at the cross and Jesus made an open spectacle of him triumphing over him there. *Psalm 20:7 KJV "Some trust in chariots, and some in horses: but we will remember the name of the LORD our God." Jesus used Scripture in Matthew 4:4 KJV*, when He was in the wilderness being tempted by the devil. Jesus lifted his shield of faith saying… *"it is written."* Then Jesus clutched the sword of the Spirit, the Word of God saying… *"It is written, Man shall not live by bread alone, but by every word that procee-deth out of the mouth of God."* Our lesson here is that if we confront the devil with the shield of faith and sword of the Spirit which is the Word of God, the enemy will flee. Jesus destroyed the enemy with the Word, and after the devil's third attempt the devil fled. We must do the same thing as Jesus and put to use our God given battle gear.

5. Guard your tongue since you preach the good news the Gospel of Christ. *"He will guard the feet of his saints" 1 Samuel 2:9 NKJV.* We are saints because we received Jesus Christ as our Lord and Savior. You are not a saint because you did this, or you did that. *"whoever guards his mouth and his tongue, Guards his soul from troubles." Proverbs 21:23 NKJV.* Jesus said it this way: *"fresh water and salt water does not come out of the same faucet."* James told us that our tongue is the hardest thing to tame, being the smallest organ of our body. *"Set a guard, O Lord, over my mouth; Keep watch over the door of my lips." Psalm 141:3 NKJV.* When I was young, I was quick with the tongue, and I prayed… "God take this away from me." As I watched my pastor who spent so much time discipling me, I began applying what he was teaching me by word and by example. Every time I asked him a question, he never answered without thinking. He would think for a few moments and then he would deliver a wise answer.

6. Guard your ways: *"I will guard my ways lest I sin with my tongue. I will restrain my mouth as with a muzzle while the wicked are in my presence. I was mute and silent, I refrained even from good, and my sorrow grew worse." Psalm 39:1-2 NASB.* We must know our frailties and guard our ways. *"LORD, who shall abide in thy tabernacle? who shall dwell in thy holy hill? He that walketh uprightly, and worketh righteousness, and speaketh the truth in his heart". Psalm 15:2 KJV.*

7. Guard what God has committed to us: Here is what Paul tells Timothy in *1 Timothy 6:20 NASB*. *"Oh Timothy, guard what has been entrusted to you, avoiding worldly and empty chatter and the opposing arguments of what is falsely called knowledge,"* thus we must guard what is committed to us. Every soldier of Christ is commissioned to preach the gospel of Jesus Christ. That is our responsibility, God gave that commission to men. God co-labors with us when we preach the Gospel. This is the most important book on the face of the earth, is the best seller of all times, there is no historical book that has even come close to it. The New Testament was written within 30 to 65 years after Jesus walked the earth. Things written of other people like Caesar and Alexander the Great were written hundreds of years after these people had lived. The Bible is the most precise writings in all of antiquity. Right here in our hands we hold the most accurate writings in history, and it is…HIS-STORY. Therefore, we must be aware that the enemy is going to try to take away from us what has been committed to us. *Luke 11:21-23 NKJV, "When a strong man, fully armed, guards his own palace, his goods are in peace. (22) "But when a stronger than he comes upon him and overcomes him, he takes from him all his armor in which he trusted and divides his spoils. (23) "He who is not with Me is against Me, and he who does not gather with Me scatters."* This so-called strong man **has been defeated by Christ,** yet he seems to be the stronger, but he is not, YOU ARE THE STRONGER IN CHRIST JESUS. Therefore, we must first bind this defeated foe from coming against the preaching of the Good

News. God is our strength to guard what he has committed to us. We need to keep our mind sharp. We must preach the Gospel because if we do not do it, who is going to? Do not allow this defeated so called strongman to overcome you. You are the stronger one through Jesus Christ. *"Greater is He that is in you than he who is in the world."* Let me give you an example. The Marianna Trent in the south Pacific Ocean is said to be seven miles deep. A man-made submarine can go no further down than three to four miles because the pressure outside the submarine is greater than the pressure inside the submarine and will crush it. Yet there are fish down there and their scales and skin are no thicker than top ocean fish. How can that be, you ask? Here is why: the pressure inside the fish is greater than the pressure outside the fish. You are that fish because greater is Christ in you than the devil in this world. I see no reason why you cannot understand this fact.

8. Guard the Sheep: Each one of us has a commission to guard our sheep. All of us have sheep committed to our charge, therefore every one of us in a way has a pastor's responsibility as a shepherd. A Pastor is a shepherd who watches over his Father's sheep. *"The thief comes only to steal and kill and destroy; I came that they may have life and have it abundantly. (11) "I am the good shepherd; the good shepherd lays down His life for the sheep. (12) "He who is a hired hand, and not a shepherd, who is not the owner of the sheep, sees the wolf coming, and leaves the sheep and flees, and the wolf snatches them and scatters them. (13) "He flees because he is a hired hand and is not concerned about the sheep. (14) "I am the good shepherd, and I know My own and My own know Me, (15) even as the Father knows Me and I know the Father; and I lay down My life for the sheep. John 10:10-15 NASB.*

As shepherds of God's sheep, we must follow Jesus as our example. A sheepfold in the Old Testament had walls approximately five feet high. On the top of it they would put briars that acted like modern day barbed wire. This sheepfold had only one door. The shepherd at nighttime would lead the sheep inside the fold and if the wolf came, he would have to jump an obstacle of a five-foot wall plus he will be pricked by the briars on the top. If he then tried to go through the door, he would have to go through the shepherd who guarded the door. Jesus is saying "I am the door". You can only get into the sheepfold through Me. I know the world does not want to hear that, but too bad, that is not what God's word says. Jesus said… *"Enter ye in by the narrow gate: for wide is the gate, and broad is the way, that leadeth to destruction, and many are they that enter in thereby." (Matthew 7:13 KJV).* Jesus is therefore saying all other religions are counterfeits. Let us look at Noah's ark having only one door, why? This is what is known as an Old Testament typology of Jesus Christ, Jesus is that one and only door to man's ark of salvation. Jesus is the genuine shepherd, and his sheep hear his voice and they enter the ark of salvation only through Him. *Psalm 23:1, "the Lord is my shepherd I shall not want." Isaiah 40:11 tells us "he will feed his flock like a shepherd; in his arms He will gather the lambs and carry them in His bosom; He will gently lead the nursing ewes."* That is what God does. *Ezekiel 34:11 NASB. "For thus says the Lord God, Indeed I myself will search for my sheep and seek them out."* When Jesus came to earth, He stepped into the role of being the Lamb of God that would take away the sins of the world. The chief quality of a shepherd is self-sacrifice. **Let me repeat what was written in a prior chapter because it is very important,** and every soldier must take it to heart and live in "agape" love and humility as a shepherd before the Lord. *John 21:15-17 says… ", when they had finished breakfast, Jesus said to Simon Peter, "Simon, son of John, do you love "agape" Me more than these?" He said to Him, "Yes, Lord; You know that I love "phileo" You." He said to him, "Tend My lambs." [16] He said to him again a second time, "Simon, son of John, do you love Me?" He said to Him, "Yes, Lord; You know that I love "phileo" You." He said to him, "Shepherd My sheep." [17] He said to him the third time, "Simon, son of John, do you love "phileo" Me?" Peter was grieved because He said to him the third time, "Do you love Me?" And he said to Him, "Lord, You know all things; You know that I love You." Jesus said to him, "Tend My sheep.* The first time Jesus addresses Peter, Jesus is using the Greek word 'agape', meaning do you love me dearly and unconditionally. Peter in return answer yes,

I love you using the Greek word "phileo", meaning a love like a brother and very fond of him. Peter is showing his newfound humility by not letting go of the word "phileo" since he knew he had prior denied him three times after being so adamant about following him all the way to the cross. He was pretty much saying no Lord, I failed you before and I will not fail you again by saying I "agape" you. This shows Peter's humility and how he was humbled. Peter finally understood. He was not going to say I love you unconditionally because he already proved he could not do that. Jesus is giving him a commission to go and teach the leaders of Israel. *Acts 4:8-12 NASB, "Then Peter, filled with the Holy Spirit, said to them, Rulers and elders of the people, if we are on trial today for a benefit done to a sick man, as to how this man has been made well, let it be known to all of you and to all the people of Israel, that by the name of Jesus Christ the Nazarene, whom you crucified, whom God raised from the dead- by this name this man stands here before you in good health. He (Jesus) is the STONE WHICH WAS REJECTED BY YOU, THE BUILDERS, but WHICH BECAME THE CHIEF CORNERSTONE. And there is salvation in no one else, for there is no other name under heaven that has been given among men by which we must be saved."*

Peter took a giant step when he began feeding the elders of Israel and the rulers of the people teaching them the good news from the Scriptures. He was bold to tell them they were rejecting the King of kings the Messiah Himself. For salvation is in Messiah alone. Peter was being called to feed, tend and protect the sheep of God's sheepfold. The call of the soldier of Christ is the same, to protect, tend, feed and serve all the sheep God has given us in our sheepfold.

Moses warned the Hebrews... *"The LORD thy God will raise up unto thee a Prophet from the midst of thee, of thy brethren, like unto me; unto him ye shall hearken; (16) According to all that thou desiredst of the LORD thy God in Horeb in the day of the assembly, saying, Let me not hear again the voice of the LORD my God, neither let me see this great fire anymore, that I die not. (17) And the LORD said unto me, They have well-spoken that which they have spoken. (18) I will raise them up a Prophet from among their brethren, like unto thee, and will put my words in his mouth; and he shall speak unto them all that I shall command him. (19) And it shall come to pass, that whosoever will not hearken unto my words which he shall speak in my name, I will require it of him." Deuteronomy 18:15-19 KJV*

Coupling that prophesy with *Acts 3:22-23 KJV* Here is what we today are told. *For Moses said, "For Moses truly said unto the fathers, A prophet shall the Lord your God raise up unto you of your brethren, like unto me; him shall ye hear in all things whatsoever he shall say unto you. (23) And it shall come to pass, that every soul, which will not hear that prophet, shall be destroyed from among the people."*

Israel was warned all along, Messiah is coming, he is greater than Moses, and when He speaks you better listen; because if you don't' it will be required of you and you will be utterly destroyed.

They knew Messiah was coming being given over 365 prophesies in the Old Testament which point to Jesus Christ and him alone, nobody else can fulfill those prophesies, not back then and not today. All through the Old Testament God had described Messiah. Let me give you an example: If I ask you to go pick up my dad at the airport and describe to you what he was going to be wearing, you surely would be able to recognize him. Dad would be wearing a black cowboy hat with a red turkey feather, yellow pants with purple socks, a white tie with orange polka dots, he would be carrying a pink duffle bag on his back and one green suitcase. I am sure you would easily recognize him. Do you see my point? Messiah would be born of a virgin in Bethlehem, a son of David, called a Nazarene, his ministry would be proceeded by a forerunner, he would bring hope to the hopeless, healing the sick, giving sight to the blind, the deaf will hear, the mute will speak, the lepers cleansed, the dead raised, he would be despised and rejected by men, led as a lamb to the slaughter, spit on, punched, nailed to a tree, bruised for our iniquity and killed, buried in a rich man's tomb, risen after three days and three nights in the heart of the earth. I hope you get my point!

Like David, the soldiers of Christ are commanded to protect God's sheep. David did just that on two occasions.

1. King Saul said to David, "you're just a boy and you're going to go against this trained giant soldier?" David replied, *"a lion came and tried to take some of my father's sheep, and I grabbed the lion by the beard struck it and killed it; a bear came and tried to take one of my father's sheep, so I struck it and killed it too."* This shows David was willing to lay down his life for his earthly father's sheep.

2. Then here comes this uncircumcised Philistine and said, *"I defy the armies of Israel this day, give me a man that we might fight together." (1 Samuel 17:10 KJV). Then said David to the Philistine, Thou comest to me with a sword, and with a spear, and with a shield: but I come to thee in the name of the LORD of hosts, the God of the armies of Israel, whom thou hast defied. (46) This day will the LORD deliver thee into mine hand; and I will smite thee, and take thine head from thee; and I will give the carcases of the host of the Philistines this day unto the fowls of the air, and to the wild beasts of the earth; that all the earth may know that there is a God in Israel." (1Samuel 17:45-46 KJV).* David is a young man who is willing to lay down his life for his heavenly Father's sheep.

He struck and killed the lion and the bear and now he removed the head from this uncircumcised Philistine who was defying the armies of Israel and taunting the name of the living God. David is certainly one young man who knows how to get the HEAD of his enemy. '*Lots Of Laughs*'. It is through faith in the LORD God of Israel. David at this point says, "I will not allow you to blaspheme the God of Israel." Of course, God was with him. Who do you think God would pick to lead his people, Israel? Wouldn't it be a man like that? The people picked Saul as king because he was tall, handsome, and humble, but that changed as time went on. God said, 'I will pick your next king.' This is the kind of man God picked, a young man with a heart for one little sheep because it was his earthly father's sheep. A good shepherd will leave the 99 to find the one. Whoever is faithful in little will be faithful in much. His son Solomon did the same thing really when he became king. God said, "ask for whatever you want" and what did Solomon say? "Give me wisdom to lead your great people Israel," Same heart, different strategy.

Soldiers of Christ are shepherds and must be of the same heart and mind as David. We need to be brave and very courageous. We must be men and women of valor, of integrity and committed soldiers like Ittai and Eleazar whom I have explained in an earlier chapter. David was just a boy, but he had faith in God and God made David the guardian over Israel as Jesus is guardian over His Father's sheep. We are told in Scripture that our Captain Jesus did not lose a single sheep that the Father has given him." Thus, we need to take our soldiering seriously, allowing no one to take your Father's sheep.

A soldier must also be watchful allowing our strength to be in God. *"Whatever is born of God overcomes the world; and this is the victory that overcomes the world, Our Faith." (1 John 5:4 NASB) He* who overcomes the world is he who believes that Jesus is the son of God. We are commanded by Scripture *(1 Corinthians 16:13 ESV) "Be watchful, stand firm in the faith, act like men, be strong."* We must serve the sheep, every one of us must be a servant like our Lord Jesus Christ. *"For even the Son of Man did not come to be served, but to serve, and to give His life a ransom for many." (Mark 10:45 NASB)* As our Captain Jesus and King David were willing to lay down their lives, we also must be willing to lay down ours. Jesus laid down His life being our greatest example. Jesus went further than that, in that while we were yet sinners, He laid down His life for us. Many people may be willing to die for a friend but not for our enemies.

"To the elders among you, I appeal as a fellow elder and a witness of Christ's sufferings who also will share in the glory to be revealed: Be shepherds of God's flock that is under your care, watching over them—not because you must, but because you are willing, as God wants you to be; not pursuing dishonest gain, but eager to serve; not lording it over those entrusted to you, but being examples to the flock." (1 Peter 5:1-3 NIV). Many people love to lord over others. A leader's duty is to serve you. Jesus was a servant

leader, and we must be servant leaders as well. In warfare your captain should be a well-loved man, because he may find some heavy consequences in the battlefield if his men do not respect him. It is always wise to be a servant leader, men will follow a leader they respect into battle. A soldier is to obey his commanding officer not questioning his reasoning. He is trained to follow no matter what the consequences, even death.

Having guard duty in the army of God is an important concern. All soldiers must be on guard at all times. *"Be alert, be on watch! Your enemy, the Devil, roams around like a roaring lion, looking for someone to devour."* *1 Peter 5:8 GNB*. Notice, the word "LIKE" here, the devil is NOT a roaring lion, he tries to fool you **acting like a** roaring lion, but you must remember he was crushed at the cross.

Food for thought: Remember, in a prior chapter, why God chose Gideon's three hundred soldiers to go the battle against the Midianites? *"And the LORD said unto Gideon, The people are yet too many; bring them down unto the water, and I will try them for thee there: and it shall be, that of whom I say unto thee, This shall go with thee, the same shall go with thee; and of whomsoever I say unto thee, This shall not go with thee, the same shall not go. {5} So he brought down the people unto the water: and the LORD said unto Gideon, Every one that lappeth of the water with his tongue, as a dog lappeth, him shalt thou set by himself; likewise everyone that boweth down upon his knees to drink. {6} And the number of them that lapped, putting their hand to their mouth, were three hundred men: but all the rest of the people bowed down upon their knees to drink water. {7} And the LORD said unto Gideon, By the three hundred men that lapped will I save you and deliver the Midianites into thine hand: and let all the other people go every man unto his place." Judges 7:4-7 KJV.*

Why, were these men chosen? Because these soldiers were watching for the enemy as they drank being always on Guard Duty. They were men who were always alert and always ready.

"THE EMPOWERED LIFE"
"Becoming a Powerful Spirit Filled Christian Soldier"

EMPOWERED BY THE HOLY SPIRIT

Chapter 7

BAPTIZED WITH FIRE

W hy does our Captain want us to live an empowered life? WHY, because it is crucial for the church today? As I look around the world, I just do not see the empowerment as it was in Biblical days. This has very much to do with being filled and baptized in the Holy Spirit. The enemy has really tripped up the church. He has set booby-traps and we have fallen for many of them.

The devil has placed fear in the church concerning the baptism of the Holy Spirit. The army of Christ is at war within themselves over this baptism. Yet it is clear within Scripture that the power did not come until the Holy Spirit fell upon the church at Pentecost. (Acts 2). Here is a good acrostic for fear: 'False Evidence Appearing Real.' The devil has caused fear and confusion over this. Baptism in simple terms means to be SATURATED and, in this case, to be saturated with the Holy Spirit. *"What? know ye not that your body is the temple of the Holy Ghost which is in you, which ye have of God, and ye are not your own? "For ye are bought with a price: therefore, glorify God in your body, and in your spirit, which are God's." 1 Corinthians 6:19-20 KJV.* Many believing soldiers of Christ Jesus are falling for the devil's lies saying… "I don't want that particular gift from God". However, Jesus told us… *"Or what man is there of you, whom if his son ask bread, will he give him a stone? {10} Or if he ask a fish, will he give him a serpent? {11} If ye then, being evil, know how to give good gifts unto your children, how much more shall your Father which is in heaven give good things to them that ask him? Matthew 7:9-11 KJV.* Since we interpret Scripture by Scripture then these verses cannot be misunderstood. *"Every good gift and every perfect gift is from above, and cometh down from the Father of lights," James 1:17 KJV.* Yet the devil has tripped up many believing soldiers and they have lost the power of the fullness of the Holy Spirit saying…"I don't want to prophesy, I don't what the word of knowledge, I don't want the discernment of spirits, I don't want to speak in tongues." Why not take every gift God wants to give you because they are all good gifts, and they bring God glory when used properly? If we do not have the baptism of the Holy Spirit, we have lost the artillery that God has for the Christian church that will level mountains. When at war the armies are always backed up by the artillery units. The baptism of the Holy Spirit is the fire power. John the Baptist told us that… *"I indeed baptize you with water unto repentance: but he (Jesus) that cometh after me is mightier than I, whose shoes I am not worthy to bear: he (Jesus) shall baptize you with the Holy Ghost, and with fire." Matthew 3:11 KJV.*

You may not have been taught about the baptism in the Holy Spirit but that does not mean it is not true. You may have to die to your old way of thinking and understand this important truth of Scripture. The soldier's enemies, the demons of darkness do not want you to know this truth since if you do it will be his utter defeat as you walk in the power of the Holy Spirit.

I believe that this is why the Christian Church has lost its dynamite power. This confusion over the baptism in the Holy Spirit has been used by the devil to defeat the soldiers of Christ, thereby eliminating the fullness of the Spirit's fire power in the soldier's life. Many believing soldiers are so fearful to receive the Spirit's gifts bestowed upon other believers. The Scriptures are clear that these gifts work together that the body of Christ might function in perfect harmony like a symphony producing beautiful music. Remember all of God's gifts are GOOD therefore why would we fear any of them.

PLEASE TAKE NOTICE of *Acts 1:4-9*, God is promising us His Holy Spirit is soon to come. Then in *Acts 2:1-4* we see the fulfillment of the God given promises and His Holy Spirit. *Acts 1:4-9 is the* fulfillment of God's promise of His Holy Spirit. *"And, being assembled together with them, commanded them that they should not depart from Jerusalem, but wait for the promise of the Father, which, saith he, ye have heard of me. {5} For John truly baptized with water; but ye shall be baptized with the Holy Ghost not many days hence. {6} When they therefore were come together, they asked of him, saying, Lord, wilt thou at this time restore again the kingdom to Israel? {7} And he said unto them, It is not for you to know the times or the seasons, which the Father hath put in his own power. {8} But ye shall receive power, after that the Holy Ghost is come upon you: and ye shall be witnesses unto me both in Jerusalem, and in all Judaea, and in Samaria, and unto the uttermost part of the earth. {9} And when he had spoken these things, while they beheld, he was taken up; and a cloud received him out of their sight." Acts 1:4-9 KJV.*

Acts 1:4 Jesus commanded the disciples not to depart from Jerusalem but to wait for the promise of the Holy Spirit from His Father. When

He comes, He will baptize {saturate} you with the Holy Spirit. Let me explain this clearly using Scripture and backed up with more Scripture.

The Baptism in the Holy Spirit is the fire power of God. Again I tell you that John the Baptist said… *"I indeed baptize you with water unto repentance: but he that cometh after me is mightier than I, whose shoes I am not worthy to bear: he shall baptize you with the Holy Ghost, and with fire:" Matthew 3:11 KJV.* If you are a born again soldier of Christ, then you have the Holy Spirit dwelling within you. In the place where the disciples were, the doors were shut and suddenly Jesus stood before them. And He showed them His hands and side. *"He breathed on them, and saith unto them, Receive ye the Holy Ghost." John 20:22 KJV.* If the disciples were not saved previously, they certainly are at this point born again. The Holy Spirit is now within them. Fifty days later we find them in the upper room basically hiding from the Roman soldiers and the Jews who were looking for them. The disciples had the Holy Spirit, but they had no courage, no power and were fearful. WHY, because the fire power had not arrived? In the morning around nine that day the promise of the Father fell **"upon"** them. Here we see the fulfillment of the promise of *Acts 1:8 KJV. "But ye shall receive power, after that the Holy Ghost is come "upon" you: and ye shall be witnesses unto me both in Jerusalem, and in all Judaea, and in Samaria, and unto the uttermost part of the earth."* Pay attention to this Greek preposition **"upon."** The Greek word is **"epi."** This **preposition means to saturate** as a sponge would be if dipped in a bucket of water and would be soaking wet just dripping due to saturation. Yes, the disciples had the Holy Spirit when Jesus breathed on them, but they were fearful and had absolutely no courage and little power because the Holy Spirit was just **"in"** them. The Greek preposition here is **"en"**. This preposition means to be **"in"** them. Hopefully, you can now understand more clearly that the empowering of the Holy Spirit is a distinct and separate experience from the indwelling Holy Spirit given at conversion. Let me ask You, you say you have the Holy Spirit but does the Holy Spirit have all of you to saturation? Let me REMIND you of what was told you earlier. Think of it this way also.

The Old Testament temple was a building and in the New Testament the temple is the believer's body. The temple building consisted of three major sections. The outer court, the Holy Place and the Holy of Holies. God's presence resided in the Ark of the Covenant located in the Holy of Holies behind the curtain. Only the High Priest was able to enter and only once per year on the Day of Atonement. When Jesus entered the temple His zeal for the Lord was shown as He overturned the money changers tables and threw them out of the temple's outer courts. The Jews had made this temple a den of thieves when it was made to be a house of prayer, where people can come and receive the LORD God as their Savior. The presence of the Holy Spirit only resided in the Holy of Holies. When Jesus died on the cross the curtain which separated the Holy of Holies from the Holy Place, and the outer courts was torn from top to the bottom. Now the presence of God, the Holy Spirit was now saturating the entire temple. Likewise, your heart is the ark now. When Jesus breathed on the disciples, they received the Holy Spirit, but His presence was only in the ark of the covenant which in the New Testament days is our heart. Since the OT temple had three parts so also, we have three parts being a triune being. We are spirit, soul, and body. *"May God himself, the God of peace, sanctify you through and through.* *"May your whole spirit, soul and body* *be kept blameless at the coming of our Lord Jesus Christ." 1 Thessalonians 5:23 NIV.* When the Holy Spirit showed up at Pentecost, He began to saturate the human body of believers with the Holy Spirit. Immediately they became valiant and courageous soldiers of Christ and began the speak in other tongues as the Spirit gave them utterance. No longer were they operating in fear but now the fire power from God. It was Passover and Jerusalem was full of people from different countries speaking many different languages. The Father is fulfilling His promise. *"But ye shall receive power,* **AFTER** *that the* **Holy Ghost is come UPON YOU***: and ye shall be witnesses unto me both in Jerusalem, and in all Judaea, and in Samaria, and unto the uttermost part of the earth. "Acts 1:8 KJV.* This is what the church is lacking, the dynamite power of God. God's dynamite power lies in the baptism of the Holy Spirit. *Acts 1:8 KJV tells us… "But ye shall receive* **power (dunamis),** *after that the Holy Ghost is come upon you: and ye shall be witnesses unto me both in Jerusalem, and in all Judaea, and in Samaria, and unto the uttermost part of the earth."* The word power here comes by the Greek word known as… **"dunamis." You are exactly right! This is where the English language gets its word DYNAMITE.**

Therefore, we must not take this lightly. On Pentecost Peter and the other 120 are no longer fearful but courageous and moving in power and fire of Almighty God. **THIS WAS THE HEBREW PENTECOST.**

Let me ask you the question again. Yes, you have the Holy Spirit but does the Holy Spirit have you?

SCRIPTURAL PROOFS OF THIS BIBLICAL TRUTH IS A MORE ACTURATE TEACHING

Apollos was a powerful preacher, but he needed to expound the Word of God more accurately. This is what the church must know and teach the Scriptures more accurately that the baptism of the Holy Spirit and fire might once again return to the church in power.

Example: *Acts 18:24-19:7 KJV. "Now a certain Jew named Apollos, an Alexandrian race, an eloquent man, came to Ephesus; and he was mighty in the scriptures. {25} This man had been instructed in the way of the Lord; and being fervent in spirit, he spake and taught accurately the things concerning Jesus, knowing only the baptism of John: {26} and he began to speak boldly in the synagogue. But when Priscilla and Aquila heard him, they took him unto them, and expounded unto him the **way of God more accurately**. {27} And when he was minded to pass over into Achaia, the brethren encouraged him, and wrote to the disciples to receive him: and when he was come, he helped them much that had believed through grace; {28} for he powerfully confuted the Jews, and that publicly, showing by the Scriptures that Jesus was the Christ."*

*Acts 19:1 KJV tells us, "And it came to pass, that, while Apollos was at Corinth, Paul having passed through the upper country came to Ephesus, and found certain disciples: {2} and he said unto them, Did ye receive the Holy Spirit when ye believed? And they said unto him, Nay, we did not so much as hear whether the Holy Spirit was given. {3} And he said, into what then were ye baptized? And they said, Into John's baptism. {4} And Paul said, John baptized with the baptism of repentance, saying unto the people that they should believe on him that should come after him, that is, on Jesus. {5} And when they heard this, they were baptized into the name of the Lord Jesus. {6} And when Paul had laid his hands upon them, **the Holy Spirit came on them; and they spake with tongues, and prophesied.** {7} And they were in all about twelve men.* Apollos was instructed and then he applied the newfound knowledge enabling the fire of God to fall upon them. We need the Holy Spirit's power today to turn this world upside down again, then and only then will the world be right side up in the Lord's eyes. As you can see from the above Scriptures, the baptism in the Holy Spirit is **A MORE ACTURATE TEACHING.**

MORE PROOF FROM SCRIPTURE:

Philip was experiencing a powerful evangelistic crusade in Samaria. Great miracles were taking place when Peter and John were sent that they might receive the Holy Spirit. *Acts 8:13-17 KJV "Then Simon himself believed also: and when he was baptized, he continued with Philip, and wondered, beholding the miracles and signs which were done. 14} **Now when the apostles which were at Jerusalem heard that Samaria had received the word of God, they sent unto them Peter and John:** {15} Who, when they were come down, prayed for them, that they might receive the Holy Ghost: {16} (For as yet he was fallen upon none of them: only they were baptized in the name of the Lord Jesus.) {17} Then laid they their hands on them, and they received the Holy Ghost."* Miracles were happening but they still needed to be baptized into the name of the Lord Jesus *{v.16}.*

PENTECOST IS GOD'S PERFECT WILL FOR THE CHURCH. I do not believe that Pentecost has ended. I will show you that virtually every people group in the New Testament had their own personal Pentecost, including yourself if you claim to be a believer. Since we interpret Scripture by Scripture there remains no doubt concerning this separate experience

WE HAVE SEEN THE HEBREW PENTECOST IN... *Acts 2:2-4 KJV And suddenly there came a sound from heaven as of a rushing mighty wind, and it filled all the house where they were sitting. {3} And there appeared unto them cloven tongues like as of fire, and it sat upon each of them. {4} And they were all filled with the Holy Ghost, and* **began to speak with other tongues, as the Spirit gave them utterance.**

NEXT, WE SEE IN SCRIPTURE THE SAMARITAN PENTECOST: *Samaria received the Holy Spirit. "Therefore they that were scattered abroad went everywhere preaching the word. {5} Then Philip went down to the city of Samaria, and preached Christ unto them. {6} And the people with one accord gave heed unto those things which Philip spake, hearing and seeing the miracles which he did. {7} For unclean spirits, crying with loud voice, came out of many that were possessed with them: and many taken with palsies, and that were lame, were healed. {8} And there was great joy in that city..." Acts 8:4-8 KJV.*

Acts 8:14-17 KJV "Now when the apostles which were at Jerusalem heard that Samaria had received the word of God, they sent unto them Peter and John: {15} Who, when they were come down, prayed for them, **that they might receive the Holy Ghost: {16} (For as yet he was fallen upon none of them: only** *they were baptized in the name of the Lord Jesus.)* **{17} Then laid they their hands on them, and** *they received the Holy Ghost.*

EVEN THE GENTILES HAD THEIR GENTILE PENTECOST AT CORNELIUS HOUSE. *"While Peter yet spake these words, the Holy Ghost fell on all them which heard the word. {45} And they of the circumcision which believed were astonished, as many as came with Peter, because that on the Gentiles also was poured out the gift of the Holy Ghost. {46} For they heard them speak with tongues, and magnify God.*

Then answered Peter, {47} Can any man forbid water, that these should not be baptized, which have received the Holy Ghost as well as we? {48} And he commanded them to be baptized in the name of the Lord. Then prayed they him to tarry certain days." Acts 10:44-48 KJV.

"When they (the Jerusalem counsel) heard these things, they held their peace, and glorified God, saying, **Then hath God also to the Gentiles granted repentance unto life.** " Acts 11:18 KJV

<u>PAUL ALSO HAD HIS PENTECOST:</u> *"And the Lord said unto him, Arise, and go into the street, which is called Straight, and enquire in the house of Judas for one called Saul, of Tarsus: for, behold, he prayeth, {12} And hath seen in a vision a man named Ananias coming in, and putting his hand on him, that he might receive his sight. {13} Then Ananias answered, Lord, I have heard by many of this man, how much evil he hath done to thy saints at Jerusalem: {14} And here he hath authority from the chief priests to bind all that call on thy name. {15} But the Lord said unto him, Go thy way: for he is a chosen vessel unto me, to bear my name before the Gentiles, and kings, and the children of Israel: {16} For I will shew him how great things he must suffer for my name's sake. {17} And Ananias went his way, and entered into the house; and putting his hands on him said, Brother Saul, the Lord, even Jesus, that appeared unto thee in the way as thou camest, hath sent me, that thou mightest receive thy sight, and be filled with the Holy Ghost. {18} And immediately there fell from his eyes as it had been scales: and he received sight forthwith, and arose, and was baptized Acts 9:11-18 KJV.*

We are assured the Apostle Paul was baptized in the Holy Spirit and fire when he himself tells us this in, *1 Corinthians 14:18 "I thank God, I speak in tongues more than you all;"*

PETER REPORTS TO US THAT <u>THE GENTILE'S HAD THEIR BAPTISM IN THE HOLY SPIRIT.</u> It was at Cornelius house that it took place. *Acts 11:13-18 And he shewed us how he had seen an angel in his house, which stood and said unto him, Send men to Joppa, and call for Simon, whose surname is Peter; {14} Who shall tell thee words, whereby thou and all thy house shall be saved. {15} And as I began to speak, the Holy Ghost fell on them, as on us at the beginning. {16} Then*

135

remembered I the word of the Lord, how that he said, John indeed baptized with water; but ye shall be baptized with the Holy Ghost. {17} Forasmuch then as God gave them the like gift as he did unto us, who believed on the Lord Jesus Christ; what was I, that I could withstand God? {18} When they heard these things, they held their peace, and glorified God, saying, then hath **God also to the Gentiles granted repentance unto life.**

HOPEFULLY, YOU HAD <u>YOUR PENTECOST</u> when you received the baptism of the HOLY SPIRIT, soon after you believed in Jesus Christ.

For me it was July 25, 1977, when Christ Jesus SAVED ME. Then exactly 3 months later on September 25, 1977, when I was baptized in water then later that same day at the alter I was BAPTIZED in the HOLY SPIRIT and received my personal Pentecost as the Holy Spirit fell **"UPON"** *me. Remember that Greek preposition* **"epi"** *which means to* **saturate.**

As you can see from the Scriptures that the empowerment of the Holy Spirit is a distinct and separate experience from receiving the Holy Spirit at conversion. From a soldier's point of view the baptism in the Holy Spirit is the artillery fire of God.

I am the pastor over a ministry known as Fervent Prayer Ministry at our church. At the end of every session, I always ask the counselee if they have been baptized in the Holy Spirit. Four out of five tell me 'Yes I have been baptized in water.' Then I begin to tell them more accurately the baptism of the Holy Spirit. Most often they say to me 'I never heard about this baptism.' My thoughts are you must be kidding!!! This is a failure on the church's part. The army of the Living God needs the artillery fire of the baptism of the Holy Spirit, and for some reason it has been hidden from the saints as the enemy creates confusion in the ranks of the Christian soldiers. Who do you think causes this confusion? We know from Scripture that God is not the author of confusion. *1 Corinthians 14:33 KJV "For* **God is not the author of confusion,** *but of* *peace, as in all churches of the saints."* James 3:16 says, *"For where envying and strife is, **there is confusion and every evil work.**"* If God is not confusions author? Then guess who is? That is right, its author is the devil, and he is boasting in laughter as the church wallows in confusion that the devil has set up as a booby trap for the saints.

I have the gift of tongues and I use it properly; I use it like Morse Code between me and God. Remember, I mentioned to you that I was a radio operator and was trained to know Morse Code in case we needed it. The devil will not hear a word of your prayer language as it is hidden by God. I have been a Christian for more than forty-four years. Some of those years were a nightmare. There were those times when I really needed the artillery power of the baptism in the Holy Spirit to edify me during those horrible times. I have always wondered why this baptism is not preached from the pulpit.

The baptism of the Holy Spirit helps us with the battle that is within us also. Our flesh is in constant battle with the Holy Spirit, and therefore the baptism of the Holy Spirit helps us with precisely that; it helps us conquer self, and it is a very important gift. *Galatians 5:17 KJV "For the flesh lusteth against the Spirit, and the Spirit against the flesh: and these are contrary the one to the other: so that ye cannot do the things that ye would."* That is conviction not condemnation. The two are in opposition to one another. This is exactly the war that goes on within us. The Apostle Paul also struggled with this. (See Romans Chapters 6 through 8). It is good to know we are not alone, for every one of us struggles with this. *Galatians 5:16 KJV* says... *"walk in the Spirit, and ye shall not fulfil the lust of the flesh."* Consequently, if we stay in the Spirit and are baptized in the Spirit we will be walking in the Spirit. Remember our carnal minds are always at war with God. It is our responsibility to get rid of the carnal mind and begin to think on a spiritual level.

How do we get the baptism of the Holy Spirit? Let me remind you again! Just like salvation, it is by faith. In *Luke 11:11-13 KJV Jesus said "If a son shall ask bread of any of you that is a father, will he give him a stone? or if he ask a fish, will he for a fish give him a serpent? {12} Or if he shall ask an egg, will he offer him a scorpion? {13} If ye then, being evil, know how to give good gifts unto your children:* **how much more shall your heavenly Father give the Holy Spirit to them that ask him?**" We are sinners yet we would not give our children something that would hurt them. It is "agape" unconditional love and just common sense, why then would God being Holy give us something that would hurt us?

So how do you get the baptism?—Just ask. Jesus becomes the baptizer not man.

HOW CAN WE LIVE THE EMPOWERED LIFE?

Get rid of self: *Luke 9:23 KJV says "If any man will come after me, let him deny himself, and take up his cross daily, and follow me."* A cross is a symbol of death; to die to yourself, therefore self must go. Jesus said… *"seek first his kingdom and his righteousness and all these things will be added unto you." Matthew 6:33 KJV.* You must remember: *"I am crucified with Christ: nevertheless I live; yet not I, but Christ liveth in me: and the life which I now live in the flesh I live by the faith of the Son of God, who loved me, and gave himself for me." Galatians 2:20 KJV.* If I have been crucified as a result, I should be dead. Occasionally, the old self likes to rear its ugly head again, but we must put him back down in submission to our Captain Jesus. In *Ephesians 4:22 KJV we are told to…"put off concerning the former conversation the old man, which is corrupt according to the deceitful lusts;"* This new man wears the battle armor of God. Someone once said "If God is going to do anything with you, you would have to get rid of self. There are some people in the Old Testament that got rid of self, let me show you a few of them.

Abraham the father of our faith was willing to leave his hometown and go to a land that he did not know at God's command. He got rid of self.

Isaac in Genesis chapter 22 was willing to lay down his life in obedience to his father. Allowing his father to bind him and place him on the altar of sacrifice. Isaac was not a child. He was most likely between

15 to 25 years old and could have easily overthrown his 115 to 125-year old father but he did not. He was willing to die in obedience to his father. Does this remind you of someone very special? That is right, our Lord and Savior Jesus Christ the Messiah of Israel. Who gave His life in obedience to His Father in order that He might redeem mankind from the penalty of sin which is eternal death? *"But God commendeth his love toward us, in that, while we were yet sinners, Christ died for us." Romans 5:8 KJV.* Isaac was rid of self as was Jesus. They were both ready to obey their Father even unto death. This picture is known as a typology in Scripture.

Joseph was willing to die to his circumstances, and because he did, God picked him up and put him on a throne, second in command only to Pharoah, in the most powerful nation in the world at that time, Egypt. He got rid of self.

Moses was willing to give up the luxury of Egypt and suffer with the children of Israel. He too was getting rid of self.

Daniel was willing to die for his faith, he was not going to bow down and worship a statute, and of course we know God delivered him. He too was getting rid of self.

Jesus was willing to do His Fathers will, He also got rid of self and willingly said… *"Father will you remove this cup from me?"* His Father answered saying, sorry Son, I cannot. To which Jesus submitted and replied, *"Thy will be done."*

Who also of us could forget, **Shadrack, Meshach and Abednego?** They also were getting rid of self.

There are those who did not get rid of self in the Old Testament.

King Saul was one of them. Do you want to be like King Saul? Then do not do what God tells you to do. God told Saul to kill all the Amalekites including all their cattle. Saul did not kill them all and on top of that he kept some of the good animals. It was an Amalekite who killed Saul. I am sure Saul would have lived a longer life if he would have just submitted to the voice and command of Almighty God.

Jonah did not want to go to Nineveh to preach repentance to the city, therefore he ran in the other direction. Finally, after being swallowed by a great fish he understood God's calling and repented and did it God's way. Then God delivered Jonah to the beach on the shore of Nineveh where he preached, and the king and city people repented because they were cut to the heart. Many people have done it their way, but if you do it your way, you are going to be very miserable in the end, you must do it God's way. Our ways are not the right way. God's way is always the right and better way.

We all who believe in Christ Jesus most definitely need the baptism in the Holy Spirit. **Do not write this off in your mind.** I just gave you Scriptural proof of the baptism in the Holy Spirit using Scripture after Scripture to back up this teaching. Study it for yourself with an open heart and you will see that you need the baptism of saturation in the Holy Spirit as does the entire church of Christ since we are the army of the Lord. We need His dynamite power to accomplish the Great Commission.

Remember *Matthew 3:11 KJV... I indeed baptize you with water unto repentance: but he that cometh after me is mightier than I, whose shoes I am not worthy to bear: **he shall baptize you with the Holy Ghost, and with fire:***

Lord, I believe just as John the Baptist has said. Baptize me in the Holy Spirit and fire to do Your will with Your power for Your glory and give to me that special gift or gifts that You would like me to have for the ministry you have chosen for me.

Please sign and date for your own remembrance.

Signature _____**Date** _____.

"OUR MARCHING ORDERS"
"Becoming a Victorious Christian Soldier"

Chapter 8

PRESENT ARMS AND CHARGE

This chapter is about our orders, why they are given and to whom. Your orders are very clear from the Captain. The primary passage is from 2 Kings 7:1-9 KJV

In this passage let me clarify that there was a famine going on in Israel. People were eating their own children and ox heads and all kinds of different weird things just to survive. So here is Elisha talking to Israel.

*"Then Elisha said, Hear ye the word of the LORD; Thus saith the LORD, Tomorrow about this time shall a measure of fine flour be sold for a shekel, and two measures of barley for a shekel, in the gate of Samaria. {2} Then a lord on whose hand the king leaned answered the man of God, and said, Behold, if the LORD would make windows in heaven, might this thing be? And he said, Behold, thou shalt see it with thine eyes, but shalt not eat thereof. {3} And there were four leprous men at the entering in of the gate: and they said one to another, Why sit we here until we die? {4} If we say, We will enter into the city, then the famine is in the city, and we shall die there: and if we sit still here, we die also. Now therefore come, and let us fall unto the host of the Syrians: if they save us alive, we shall live; and if they kill us, we shall but die. {5} And they rose up in the twilight, to go unto the camp of the Syrians: and when they were come to the uttermost part of the camp of Syria, behold, there was no man there. {6} For the Lord had made the host of the Syrians to hear a noise of chariots, and a noise of horses, even the noise of a great host: and they said one to another, Lo, the king of Israel hath hired against us the kings of the Hittites, and the kings of the Egyptians, to come upon us. {7} Wherefore they arose and fled in the twilight, and left their tents, and their horses, and their asses, even the camp as it was, and fled for their life. {8} And when these lepers came to the uttermost part of the camp, they went into one tent, and did eat and drink, and carried thence silver, and gold, and raiment, and went and hid it; and came again, and entered into another tent, and carried thence also, and went and hid it. {9} Then they said one to another, **We do not well: this day is a day of good tidings, and we hold our peace: if we tarry till the morning light, some mischief will come upon us: now therefore come, that we may go and tell the king's household.**" 2 Kings 7:1-9 KJV*

This Syrian officer did not believe Elisha or the Word of the LORD. He probably thought 'God can't do that, and that is one of the things I tried to drive home in chapter 3. "Did you forget who God is?" This Samaritan officer obviously forgot or did not have a relationship with Jehovah. It's written in *Isaiah 55:11 KJV* "*So shall my word be that goeth forth out of my mouth: it shall not return unto me void, but it shall accomplish that which I please, and it shall prosper in the thing whereto I sent it."* The word was sent forth and this Samaritan officer did not believe it. The officer was in doubt.

'Thus saith the LORD,' *"The heaven is my throne, and the earth is my footstool: where is the house that ye build unto me?"* Isaiah 66:1 KJV

We must get out of this box mentality of who God is, who Jesus is; and this Samaritan officer was in that box because he did not believe. We realize from *John 1:1 KJV...* that Jesus is the creator, *"In the beginning was the Word and the Word was with God and the Word was God."* *'In the beginning,'* the Greek word used is 'arche' which means **BEYOND THE BEGINNING OF TIME.** Before the beginning of time was Jesus, He is the creator. *Colossians 1:16-17 KJV* tells us *"For by him were all things created, that are in heaven, and that are in earth, visible and invisible, whether they be thrones, or dominions, or principalities, or powers: all things were created by him, and for him: And he is before all things, and by him all things consist."*

Hence, this Samaritan officer will receive the consequence of not believing the Word of the LORD. He was going to see it come to pass but he was not going to be able to eat it.

These four leprous men went down to the Syrian camp knowing they were going to die one way or the other. They reasoned amongst themselves and said if we are going to die, we may as well die with a full belly than an empty one. They went down and to their surprise the Syrians had left. The Lord had caused the Syrians to hear the sound of thundering horses and chariots and they took off as fast as they could leaving their spoil behind. It is a lot easier and faster to travel without anything weighing you down. The lepers came into the camp and saw no one there. They began eating and drinking, they got rich, and they knew they were wrong. Sometimes in this world us Christian soldiers, we eat, we drink, we get rich, and we forget that we are doing wrong, The Christian soldier has prior orders from our Captain Jesus that are of **first importance.** We need to share the good news and that is what these lepers concluded. They said to themselves, **"We are not**

doing right, this is a day of good news" and we remain silent." For the Christian soldier, this is a day of good news. We have the good news and yet many of us remain silent. Many people today are in the Valley of Decision and our orders are these… **GO and TELL all the world that Jesus is Risen.** The penalty for our sin has been PAID IN FULL. Our Captains orders are recorded in *Matthew 28:19-20 KJV* "*Go ye therefore, and teach all nations, baptizing them in the name of the Father, and of the Son, and of the Holy Ghost: {20} Teaching them to observe all things whatsoever I have commanded you: and, lo, I am with you alway, even unto the end of the world."*

Mark 16:15 KJV "***Go Ye into all the world and preach the gospel to every creature."*** There is a promise attached to going as told in *Acts 1:8 KJV* "*But ye shall receive power, after that the Holy Ghost is come upon you: and ye shall be witnesses unto me both in Jerusalem, and in all Judaea, and in Samaria, and unto the uttermost part of the earth."* In *Luke 24:45-49* here is Jesus again saying, *"Then opened he their understanding, that they might understand the scriptures, {46} And said unto them, Thus it is written, and thus it behoved Christ to suffer, and to rise from the dead the third day: {47} And that repentance and remission of sins should be preached in his name among all nations, beginning at Jerusalem. {48} And ye are witnesses of these things. {49} And, behold, I send the promise of my Father upon you: but tarry ye in the city of Jerusalem, until ye be endued with power from on high."* Remember the prophet Gad told David that it was time to get out of the stronghold, likewise Jesus sends us out of the stronghold. Remember, the soldier of Christ's stronghold is the church. Occasionally, after we are sent out by the Holy Spirit, we are to recover and strengthen ourselves as we go back into the stronghold. We come to church to be assembled to draw strength, encouragement, and exhortation from the Holy Spirit and one another. In the stronghold we hear the word of God and grow deeper in the grace and knowledge of the Lord. We are to go out of the stronghold to preach the gospel yet not to get into the worldly entanglements. Our orders…Preach the Good News" to the world, Christ is Risen. The only problem is that many

Christian soldiers have retreated to the stronghold and have stayed there, forgetting the lost that are in the valley of decision. They have become comfortable in complacency and are now ignoring the fact that they are soldiers who fight for the souls of lost men and women.

'The lepers said amongst themselves if we wait till morning it will be too late.' The morning light has come, and if we wait too long it will also be too late. We are expected to obey our Captain's orders, we are expected to go out there and do it, DO WHAT? GO and TELL Christ is Risen. This charge is laid to every Christian soldier. We may not have the gift of evangelism like Billy Graham, but we all must evangelize. Our Marching Orders from our Captain, the Lord Jesus are to Go and Tell. Therefore, get out, Forward March into the world with the good news. Jesus is counting on us. If every Christian kept their mouths shut then the gospel would not be told, and we would not be doing right. The light has already come, Jesus being the light of the world, and we are not supposed to hide the light under a little basket, (Matthew 5) therefore, do not hide your light under a bushel.

As a result, the lepers said to one another, *"therefore come let us GO and TELL."* Remember your first love Jesus then GO and TELL. Now is the time to fall back in love with Jesus, realize what He has done for us once again and go and tell the good news. Remember what Jesus told the women on resurrection Sunday? *Matthew 28:10 KJV... "Then said Jesus unto them, Be not afraid:* **GO TELL** *my brethren that they go into Galilee, and there shall they see Me."*

"Prepare for war! Wake up the mighty men, (that's us) *"Let all the men of war draw near, Let them come up. "Beat your plowshares into swords and your pruning hooks into spears; Let the weak say, 'I am strong.' "Assemble and come, all you nations, and gather together all around. Cause your mighty ones to go down there, O Lord. "Let the nations be wakened, and come up to the Valley of Jehoshaphat; for there I will sit to judge all the surrounding nations. Put in the sickle, for the harvest is ripe. Come, go down; for the winepress is full, the vats overflow—for their wickedness is great."* **Multitudes, multitudes in the valley of decision!** *For the day of the Lord is near in the valley*

of decision. The sun and moon will grow dark, and the stars will diminish their brightness. The Lord also will roar from Zion, and utter His voice from Jerusalem; the heavens and earth will shake; But the Lord will be a shelter for His people, and the strength of the children of Israel. "So you shall know that I am the Lord your God, Dwelling in Zion My holy mountain. Then Jerusalem shall be holy, and no aliens shall ever pass through her again." Joel 3:9-17 NKJV

"Come, go down; for the winepress is full, the vats overflow—for their wickedness is great:" The world and **THE CHURCH MUST REPENT, RETURN AND FORSAKE SIN**, but as I mentioned earlier, the world looks at the church and says, 'when are they going to repent.' They have this and that going on, divorce and adultery, fornication, iniquities, transgressions, homosexuality, unbelief and many other sins. It is time for the church to clean ourselves in the shed blood of Christ, then get rid of self and put on the breast plate of Christ's righteousness and the belt of truth again. When they see the church repenting of our sins then they are going to want to be part of it, and that will be when we will be recognized as the lights in the world. *"For it is time for judgment to begin with the household of God; if it begins with us first, what will be the outcome for those who do not obey the gospel of God?" James 4:17 NASB*

Billions of people are in a valley of decision. Every one of us is faced with a decision, "Is there a God or not and is Jesus the long awaited Messiah?" It took me six years before I responded to my wake-up call even though I knew that I knew Jesus was calling me to enlist in His Heavenly Army. I now understood and believed that Jesus was God's Beloved Son. This is every soldier of Christ's commission to… *"Proclaim this among the nations: Prepare for war!* We are not talking war with carnal weapons but rather heavenly weapons.

Once again, we soldiers of Christ must remember…*Joel 3:14 KJV,* **"Multitudes, multitudes in the valley of decision!"** *For the day of the Lord is near in the valley of decision."* Our orders are to have a life of witnessing because the field is ripe for harvest, and there are multitudes in this valley of decision. Our orders are to go and make disciples, rescuing them before they go into the abyss. This is so important for us to hear and obey. We must keep our eyes, and ears and our hearts open to whomever God puts before us who is willing to hear and in doing so Gospel seeds are planted. You can say, do you know that Jesus loves you? If somebody reaps him ten years from now, you have a part in that harvest in that person's salvation. The Scriptures say that the sower and the reaper are the same; it is God who brings the increase. You may not become a great evangelist, but you need to lead and equip people to go out and do it. When I was in business for twenty some years in Pennsylvania, there were many people that came to the Lord. Many knew I was a Christian, and those who were hungry would ask me about God. People would ask me to pray for them and I would. I had many employees over the years and there is only one that I know of who did not get saved. Your business can be a vehicle to tell the good news wherever you go. And if we do not, like the lepers, we would not be doing right. Your sword must not be in its sheath all the time. Much good is going to be done when you remove your sword (the Word of God) from its sheath. Remember *Romans 13:11-12 NKJV "And do this, knowing the time, that now it is high time to awake out of sleep; for now our salvation is nearer than when we first believed. {12} The night is far spent, the day is at hand. Therefore let us cast off the works of darkness, and let us put on the armor of light."* Remember again, Isoroku Yamamoto the Japanese Admiral, who was congratulated for his great victory at Pearl Harbor. He was credited with these few words 'I fear that we have awaken a sleeping giant.' IF THE CHURCH WOULD WAKE UP, WE ARE THAT SLEEPING GIANT. It is time for us to wake up. If we wake up, we are going to see a great harvest in the world. You must find out what the Lord has put in your heart then go and do it.

In America, it seems that the spiritual climate is decreasing rapidly. We see and hear of people dying without Christ and yet many believers have become numb. It seems as if many Christian soldiers could care less. After all they are saved from the righteous wrath to come. It is all about me. **The selfish trinity of me, myself and I is reigning in the lives of many believers.** Their prayer is mostly about themselves. Bless me Lord is a prayer they commonly pray. They no longer ache and shed tears for the perishing. They fill up on the Word of God but very seldom apply what they hear from their preacher as he expounds on the Word of God. If you were in the US Army and did not apply what your drill sergeant taught you, you would be doing plenty of pushups and peeling many a potato. Jesus had compassion on everyone, the crippled, the lepers, the blind, the sick, the lost etc. Without compassion the Christian soldier is at a great loss. We must have compassion for people for they are God's creation. We must love them. We must care for where they will spend eternity. As a soldier of Christ let us leave no man behind.

What shocks me most is…Soldiers are trained to rise to the trumpet sound every morning, but now they can't even get out of bed for church. Jesus died for you, and you can't even get out of bed? Let me remind you, the trumpet has already sounded, it is time to get about doing what our Captain has commanded us. One of our Captain's commands is to… *"Not forsake the assembling of ourselves together, as the manner of some is; but exhorting one another: and so much the more, as ye see the day approaching. Hebrews 10:25 KJV.* If you have regressed to this place, you are no longer acting as a disciplined soldier.

SEVEN THINGS ABOUT GOD'S WARRIORS:

1. God's soldiers position themselves for victory: they stand firm and after all that they've done to stand, they stand firm, therefore. In other words, it is doubly emphatic, do all you can to stand and then stand further, therefore. The God of all grace, after we suffer a while, he will perfect, establish, settle us and strengthen us. He is going to perfect us completely, He is going to completely restore us, He is going to establish us, in other words He is going to set it up or establish us to be strong and courageous like he did with Joshua. To strengthen us is to reinforce us; He will mature us and complete us.

2. God's soldiers pick themselves up in times of defeat: We accept the defeat as long as we know that God was in the battle. But if we do fall, the Scriptures are clear the righteous will never be forsaken. A righteous man may fall seven times and rise again, he may be hard pressed on every side yet not crushed, he may be perplexed but not in despair, he may be persecuted but not forsaken, stricken down but not destroyed. In other words, our defeat only strengthens the Christian soldier for future battles. In these times we learn how to read the Bible, meditate on it, digest the word of God, and it becomes our joy and our salvation. Then we can grow more in the Lord and fall in love with him. That is what the trying times do to us. So do not feel bad if you feel like you were defeated, you are not. The war is already won, even though you may have lost a little fire fight.

3. God's soldiers defend their ground: They are alert, and they stand firm in faith. They act like soldiers because they are trained soldiers, they are men of God strong in faith. (See *1 Corinthians* 16:13). Soldiers stand when is easy to run, David could have run from Goliath or the bear, instead, David ran at Goliath for all the right reasons, Goliath mocked the name of the living God and God brought victory. When the enemy or just life itself comes against you, just stand fast, stand strong.

4. God's soldiers take back what the enemy has stolen: This is the heritage of the servants of the Lord. *"No weapon that is formed against thee shall prosper; and every tongue that shall rise against thee in judgment thou shalt condemn. This is the heritage of the servants of the LORD, and their righteousness is of me, saith the LORD."* This verse is from *Isaiah 54:17 KJV.* You are able to personalize this verse for yourself, simply put your name in the appropriate place. God's soldiers have been given the command to take back the kingdom. *"I kept looking, and that horn was waging war with the saints and overpowering them {22} until the Ancient of Days came and judgment was passed in favor of the saints of the Highest*

One, and the time arrived when the saints took possession of the kingdom. Daniel 7:21-22 NASB 'Then the sovereignty, the dominion and the greatness of all the kingdoms under the whole heaven will be given to the people of the saints of the Highest One; His kingdom will be an everlasting kingdom, and all the dominions will serve and obey Him.' Daniel 7:27 NASB. For the soldier of Christ {the saints of the Most High}, it should not be about money, cars, houses, or businesses, it is about people in the valley of decision; and it is about carrying out the Master's orders. As you can see from the above verses in Daniel Chapter 7 there is a war going on throughout the ages. I call it the War of All Ages that is still raging. A short summary of this chapter would go something like this. The big horn and the little horns were blaspheming the LORD as He reigns being the Ancient of Days (God the Father). Then comes the Son of man who is given dominion riding on a cloud. The horn was making war with the saints and prevailing until the Ancient of Days (God the Father) pronounced judgment from the throne and His verdict is that He rules in favor of the saints of the Most High. Then the time came for the saints to possess the kingdom. Christian soldier **THAT TIME IS NOW!** Listen to what Jesus said, *Matthew 11:12 KJV "And from the days of John the Baptist until now the kingdom of heaven suffereth violence, and the violent take it by force."* NOW IS THE TIME TO TAKE POSSESSION OF THE KINGDOM. Remember: *Daniel Chapter 7:22 **"Until the Ancient of days came, and judgment was given to the saints of the Most High; and the time came that the saints possessed the kingdom."***

5. **God's soldiers refuse to be overcome:** We are more than conquerors, because Jesus has already conquered, and that makes us more than a conqueror. *"For a righteous man falleth seven times, and riseth up again" Proverbs 24:16 KJV.* When the righteous man falls, he gets back up. If you fall flat on your face, the first position to getting up is to get on your knees. God is your first line of defense hears your prayers before they even come out of your mouth. The victorious soldier of Christ refuses to be overcome. There is no white flag for a Christian, and we

do not retreat, when you retreat there is no protection to cover your back. Why retreat then, press on? If you are wearing the armor of God, it will fit you perfectly. it is not encumbering. Jesus' yoke is easy, and my burden is light says the Lord. There is no white flag for the Christian. Even God when he goes into battle puts on his armor of righteousness; he puts on righteousness like a breastplate, and his helmet is on His head, See *Isaiah 59:17-19.* God's soldiers seek first his kingdom, some Christians get so wrapped up in the cares of this world. I have done it myself many times. Jesus said first seek His kingdom and His righteousness and all these things will be added on to you. He is not talking about money; He is talking about welfare. We need to put Jesus first, we need to yield our will, our rights, and our control to him. Therefore, if any man be in Christ, he is a new creature. It is God then that controls him. If I have been crucified with Christ it is no longer I who live but Christ that lives in me. That means I am dead, and He should saturate my being. Yielding to Him is what the Lord expects of his soldiers.

6. God's soldiers speak life: *"Life and death are in the power of the tongue and those who love it will eat its fruit."* Therefore, we need to speak life. Here is the key verse: *Psalm 107:2 KJV "let the redeemed of the Lord say so."* Captain Jesus has redeemed us from the hand of the enemy. We speak life into people as we present the good news to them about Jesus. Just give your testimony saying to them, "once I was lost and now, I am found. Once I was a drunk and now, I am not, once I was a druggie and now, I am not." When in doubt, give your testimony. The Apostle Paul gave his many times in the book of Acts.

A soldier of God is disciplined, consistent, teachable, willing to serve, he is trustworthy, responsible, and hungry for the things of God. God can trust him to GO and TELL the good news. He is always looking to share his faith with others.

7. God's soldiers maintain God's priorities: *Micah 6:8 KJV "He hath shewed thee, O man, what is good; and what doth the LORD requires of thee, but to do justly, and to love mercy, and to walk humbly with thy God?"*

He is submissive to authority: The centurion recognized it in Jesus. He said, "you don't have to come to my house, one word from you and my servant will be healed." A Christian soldier carries out our orders from the Captain. Therefore, carry out the good news which are His marching orders to mankind. *He may be troubled on every side, yet not distressed; he is perplexed, but not in despair; Persecuted, but not forsaken; cast down, but not destroyed;* See *2 Corinthians 4:8-11.* He does all things well, he learns humility, which is the biggest virtue of a Christian soldier. *You must remember God the Father said...*

"*But to this one I will look, To him who is **humble** and **contrite of spirit**, and **who trembles at My word**.*" *Isaiah 66:2 NASB.*

God's soldiers are courageous in faith, strong, brave, and daring like David, Eliezer, Ittai, etc.

Some people in this world trust in chariots or horses, they trust in their boss, their parents, money, drugs and in all kinds of things, but not the Christian soldier. We trust in the name of the Lord God. In His name demons tremble, foundations shake, people are saved, healed, and delivered.

Let us look back and review quickly what we have encountered in these eight chapters thus far? This instruction without your application will keep you in the frustration you are now living.

IT IS NOW TIME FOR YOUR CHANGE.

KNOWING YOU CAN DO ALL THINGS THROUGH CHRIST WHO STRENGTHENS YOU.
{See Philippians 4:13}

Let us review...

Chapter 1 of this book you are reading, *Joel 3:9* is telling us *to "proclaim the good news to the nations and let them come up."* This tells us that the nations must make an **"ABOUT FACE."** We all need to make an

"ABOUT FACE." repenting of and forsaking our sins. This applies to the backsliding Christian as well as the unbelieving. The first group are those who do not have a relationship with Messiah. Then the second group are those that have a personal relationship yet are seemingly backsliding. You must fall back in love with Jesus and remember what he did for us. He could have stayed in heaven and have Michael and Gabriel feed him grapes, but no, He got off his throne and came down here to be abused and killed by men to save your soul.

Chapter 2 "Prepare for War," this is talking of **"BASIC TRAINING."** We must be trained for the basics of spiritual warfare, not physical warfare. We fight with the Sword of the Spirit, and every time we use this sword it gets sharper and sharper, not duller, and duller as carnal swords do. Every time the physical soldiers went out to battle, they had to spend the night sharpening their swords. But every time the soldier of Christ uses the Sword of the Living God, this Sword becomes sharper and sharper as we learn to handle the Sword accurately. Every time we lift the shield of faith **"it is written"**, our arms get stronger from constantly standing up in faith, as Jesus did in the wilderness. He would lift His shield saying, **"it is written."** Then taking His sword of the Spirit He would use Scripture to refute the enemy, *"Get thee hence, Satan: for it is written, Thou shalt worship the Lord thy God, and him only shalt thou serve."* Therefore, as we use the sword, the word of God, we are growing sharper and more accurately controlling our Sword of the Spirit.

Chapter 3 *"Wake Up Mighty Men";* Joel 3:9, here we speak of **"REVEILLE."** It is now time to be wide awake and ready for battle. Wake up soldier, the light has already come. Jesus who is the light of the world, came into the world as prophesied the first time and He is about to come a second time very soon. We, the soldiers of Christ must gather in formation. The next trumpet is about to sound, and we must get busy and obey our Captains Commission *"to go therefore and make disciples of all nations baptizing them in the name of the Father, the Son, and the Holy Spirit".* We must be ready to be sent outside the stronghold as equipped soldiers with our battle gear intact. Again, these instruments I am talking about are not instruments of physical war, but spiritual warfare. We know that we are weak but through God we become strong when we learn how to use the equipment that He has given us. Thus, *"we can do all things through Christ"*. We become strong as we use the Armor of God. I have repeated this many times in this book because it is of utmost importance. Always remember, there is nowhere in Scripture where it tells us to take off any part of the Armor of God. If you take off the helmet of salvation the devil can put doubt in your mind. We have the breastplate of righteousness, some of us think we can live an ungodly life, but we are told to be holy as God is holy, we are not going to be perfect, **God does not expect perfection He expects progress from us**. If we take off the belt of truth we are going to be exposed and become a target for the enemy because the belt of truth holds the weapons. It holds the sword; it holds the bow and arrow quiver intact. If we take off the shoes of salvation, then consider why do the Scriptures say, *"blessed are the feet of those who bring the tidings of good news"?* Many a soldier have been taken out of the battle by the enemy, attacking the message their feet carry into the battlefield which is Jesus is Risen". Therefore, we are told to always keep our sandals on. The enemy will place glass and sharp metal shavings in the battlefield to cut and damage your feet and remove you from the fight. *"There are multitudes, multitudes in the valley of decision"*, and it has been that way for centuries. We must therefore protect our feet. *Joel 3:13 KJV tells us…" Put ye in the sickle, for the harvest is ripe."* Then Jesus comes saying… *"the field is ripe for harvest; the workers are few."* The plan to win this world is effective, but the soldier of Christ must step into his commission and perform his duty.

Chapter 4, Not only have you been trained in the basics of spiritual warfare, but you have been trained in your specialty gift. **A.I.T. ("ADVANCED INSTRUCTIONAL TRAINING)."** You have learned how to use your specialty gifts for spiritual warfare. You have… *"Beaten your plowshares into swords, and your pruninghooks into spears: let* *the weak say, I am strong." See Joel 3:10.* Now you are ready to get outside the stronghold of the church and go to battle and win the lost sheep. You have turned around and made an **ABOUT FACE** and are now following your Captain Jesus Christ. You were trained in the **BASICS.** You have been called to attention at **REVEILLE** and you have also been trained in your specialty gift at **A.I.T. (Advanced Instructional Training).** Now it is time to **FORWARD MARCH** going into the world to preach the Good News.

Chapter 5, *Joel 3:11… "Assemble and come, all you nations, and gather together all around":* We are being assembled together because is time for the soldier of Christ to "**FORWARD MARCH**". Jesus sent us out two thousand years ago on a recon mission. He said, *"go and make disciples"* this is our mission because we are now in formation, we are now equipped, and we are ready to march in unity outside of the stronghold. *"Cause your mighty ones to go down there, O Lord":* Who are the mighty ones? These are the ones empowered by the Holy Spirit. This refers to when Jesus told the disciples to go and wait in Jerusalem for the promise of the Father, the Holy Spirit. REMEMBER: Peter and the hundred and twenty in the upper room received the power of the Holy Spirit, fifty days after Christ's resurrection. Zachariah said it best *"not by might nor by power but by your Spirit says the Lord."* We are weak, but God is strong, and it is by the power of His Spirit that these things are done, and we become mighty ones. We cannot fight spiritual things with carnal weapons. *"For although we walk in the flesh, we do not war according to the flesh. For the weapons of our warfare are not carnal but mighty in God for pulling down strongholds, casting down arguments and every high thing that exalts itself against the knowledge of God, bringing every thought into captivity to the obedience of Christ,"* 2 Corinthians 10:3-5 NKJV. Therefore, the empowered life comes through the Holy Spirit as we use the gifts of the Spirit and Forward March into this dark world.

Chapter 6 speaks to us of "GUARD DUTY." The soldier of Christ must be awake to guard his life. You must Guard your heart because is the wellspring of life. You must also guard your spirit because is the part of us that said yes to Jesus. It is important to be awakened and guard these things. You are a triune being as is the LORD. *1 Thessalonians 5:23 KJV "And the very God of peace sanctify you wholly; and **I pray God your whole spirit and soul and body be preserved blameless** unto the coming of our Lord Jesus Christ." "Let the nations be wakened, and come up to the Valley of Jehoshaphat;*

*For there I will sit to judge all the surrounding nations." Joel 3:12 NKJV. "...the **LORD will be a shelter for His people,** and the strength of the children of Israel." Joel 3:16b NKJV.* Captain Jesus will protect you. That is His part. You also have a responsibility to protect yourself from things that can bring you down. The lust of the flesh, the lust of the eyes and the boastful pride of life are a few that you must guard against. See *1 John 2:15-16.*

Chapter 7 confirms to us that all believing soldiers **have the Holy Spirit "IN" them.** {Greek word "EN"}. Yet are saved from the wrath of God. But the **empowering of the Holy Spirit we receive when the Holy Spirit comes UPON us** {Greek word "EPI"}. *Acts 1:8* being fulfilled in Pentecost on *Acts 2:4.* Remember the disciples had the Holy Spirit in them when Jesus breathed on them; in *John 20:22* resurrection Sunday evening, yet they were powerless and feared for their lives for 50 days until Pentecost. When the Holy Spirit came UPON them their fear was taken away and they began to preach the Gospel with all boldness, *"Let the weak say, 'I am strong."* For now, they have been saturated with the dynamite power of the Living God. Where does your strength and power lie? That's right it is in the power of the Holy Spirit given to each of us when we are baptized in the Holy Spirit as in the days of Pentecost. I have news for you believing Christian soldier. **PENTECOST HAS NOT ENDED.** The book of Acts has no end yet. It simply implies that the preaching goes on with the men and women who will not stop preaching the gospel throughout the years to follow. See *Acts 28:30-31 KJV "And Paul dwelt two whole years in his own hired house, and received all that came in unto him, (31) Preaching* *the kingdom of God, and teaching those things which concern the Lord Jesus Christ, with all confidence, no man forbidding him."* The preaching of the kingdom is what the Lord Jesus commissioned us to continue until He comes again. The baptism in the Holy Spirit and His power is what we will need to accomplish the task placed before us. *Mark 16:15 KJV...*" *And he said unto them, Go ye into all the world, and preach the gospel to every creature. {16} He that believeth and is baptized shall be saved; but he that believeth not shall be damned."*

LET ME REPEAT SINCE THIS IS VERY IMPORTANT.

You must take note and remember the disciples were hiding out from the Romans and the Jewish leaders until they were baptized on high in the Holy Spirit at Pentecost. Then power began. *Acts 1:8 KJV "But **ye shall receive power, after that the Holy Ghost is come upon you:** and ye shall be witnesses unto me both in Jerusalem, and in all Judaea, and in Samaria, and unto the uttermost part of the earth."*

John the Baptist preached this to us... *"I indeed baptize you with water unto repentance: but he that cometh after me is mightier than I, whose shoes I am not worthy to bear: he shall baptize you with the Holy Ghost, and with fire: Matthew 3:11 NKJV."* When you are baptized in the Holy Spirit, it is Jesus who baptizes you and not a mere man. Notice that Jesus baptizes you with the Holy Spirit and fire. *Acts 1:8 KJV "But ye shall receive power, after that the Holy Ghost is come upon you:"*

After the 120 were baptized in the Holy Spirit no one could shut them up. They were fearless and full of courage. No one could stop them because now they were saturated with the Holy Spirit's power. Their cup was full to the overflowing to everyone who heard the Word they preached.

Chapter 8 *"Put in the sickle for the harvest is ripe:"* We must gather the harvest before it is to late to pick. Our orders are to GO and TEL L all the world that Jesus is Risen. **PRESENT ARMS which is to say use your God given gifts to apply in the battle for the harvest, then CHARGE quickly and reap while ripe before the fruit rots.** The salvation of men lies in the balance and if we do not tell them then who will? Jesus gave us this charge before He ascended into heaven. His work on earth is done, and now Captain Jesus is counting on us. Without us the plan just falls. He started with the eleven disciples, and they changed the world. They turned the world upside down and the same can be done with us today. It is time to awaken out of our sleep and go out and do the same thing we did at first, **falling back in love with Jesus and remember who he is**, and doing what we did at first because we sometimes forget!!

Dear Christian soldier of Christ. You have been **enlisted in God's army**. You have **repented and have forsaken** your sins. You have been **trained to use your God given spiritual weapons** and you have also **been trained in a specialized field**. The **Captain has now gotten your attention** and you are **forward marching** outside of the church stronghold when necessary. You are always **pulling guard duty by being watchful** for enemy attacks and you are **guarding your heart** and soul from any enemy confrontations. You have been **empowered by the Holy Spirit** of the Living God. **YOUR ORDERS** from Captain Jesus are to **present arms and charge into the harvest field** for there are multitudes, multitudes in the Valley of Decision.

OUR CAPTAIN JESUS CHRIST HAS GIVEN HIS CHRISTIAN SOLDIERS (the church) OUR MARCHING ORDERS. Here they are simply put. *"And Jesus came and spake unto them, saying, All power is given unto me in heaven and in earth.* "Go ye therefore, and teach all nations, baptizing them in the name of the Father, and of the Son, and of the Holy Ghost: {20} Teaching them to observe all things whatsoever I have commanded you: and, lo, I am with you always, even unto the end of the world. Matthew 28:18-20 KJV.*

If you are not obeying God in Christ's commands, then like the four lepers.

You *are not doing right: this day is a day of good news, and you are remaining silent: if you wait until the morning light, multitudes will be lost forever.*

NOW THEREFORE "GO AND TELL" THEM, TO "COME AND SEE" THAT, CHRIST IS RISEN INDEED, NOW IT IS TIME TO "GO AND TELL" "BECAUSE HE LIVES, YOU CAN LIVE ALSO."

"That if thou shalt <u>confess with thy mouth the Lord Jesus</u>, and shalt <u>believe in thine heart</u> that God hath raised him from the dead, thou shalt be saved. For <u>with the heart man believeth</u> unto righteousness; and <u>with the mouth confession is made unto salvation.</u>" Romans 10:9-10 KJV

NOW, therefore heed your Captain and carry out His orders – "ABOUT FACE" and REPENT. RE-UP now and RETURN to the LORD'S Camp.

Signature _____ Date _____.

ACKNOWLEDGEMENTS

I would like to first give thanks to my wife, Lisette Trapani whose patience and support enabled this teaching.

To my daughter-in-law, Barbara Afanador. Thank you for helping to finalize my vision through creative images on the front and back cover as well as the images throughout each chapter.

Claudia Palo, I can't thank you enough for your countless hours of reviewing, typing and editing Chapters 1 through 8.

Reijo Palo, thank you so much for your time spent on some design ideas and input that I found very useful in this endeavor.

Chaplain James Houchens, for checking Bible verses and their references. Every verse has purpose in every person's life. Thank you for helping me to capture, verify and edit the biblical reference. If anyone would like to reach out to Chaplain Houchens, he can be reached at travelministry@aol.com

To Late Ms. Linda Sapienza Casaceli, I send many thanks to you for typing Chapters 1 through 4. We know you are home with the Lord. Knowing that you helped with this book is something my heart will never forget.

NOTES

NOTES

NOTES

NOTES

NOTES

NOTES